ECONOMIC HISTORY

AGRARIAN CHANGE AND ECONOMIC DEVELOPMENT

AGRICULTURE

AGRARIAN CHANGE AND ECONOMIC DEVELOPMENT

The historical problem

Edited by

E.L. JONES AND S.J. WOOLF

Routledge
Taylor & Francis Group

LONDON AND NEW YORK

First published in 1969

Published in 2006 by
Routledge
2 Park Square, Milton Park, Abingdon, Oxfordshire OX14 4RN
711 Third Avenue, New York, NY 10017

First issued in paperback 2014

Routledge is an imprint of the Taylor and Francis Group, an informa business

© 1969 E.L. Jones and S.J. Woolf

The publishers have made every effort to contact authors and copyright
holders of the works reprinted in the *Economic History* series. This has not
been possible in every case, however, and we would welcome
correspondence from those individuals or organisations we have been
unable to trace.

These reprints are taken from original copies of each book. In many cases
the condition of these originals is not perfect. The publisher has gone to
great lengths to ensure the quality of these reprints, but wishes to point out
that certain characteristics of the original copies will, of necessity, be
apparent in reprints thereof.

British Library Cataloguing in Publication Data
A CIP catalogue record for this book
is available from the British Library

Agrarian Change and Economic Development
ISBN 0-415-37696-3 (volume)
ISBN 0-415-37652-1 (subset)
ISBN 0-415-28619-0 (set)
ISBN13: 978-1-138-86167-1 (pbk)
ISBN13: 978-0-415-37696-9 (hbk)

Routledge Library Editions: Economic History

*Agrarian Change and
Economic Development*

Agrarian Change and Economic Development

The Historical Problems

Edited by
E. L. JONES
and
S. J. WOOLF

METHUEN & CO LTD

First published 1969 by Methuen & Co. Ltd,
11 New Fetter Lane, London E.C.4
Introduction © 1969 by E. L. Jones and S. J. Woolf

416   12240 **X**

Distributed in the U.S.A.
by Barnes & Noble Inc.

Contents

Preface

This volume, like the seminar which gave rise to it, is concerned with the role of agriculture in the 'western model' of economic development. The choice of the 'western model' needs no explanation, given the decisive part it has played in generating the modern world's unequal economic structure. Agriculture has until recent times been the world's dominant activity and must inevitably be a major item on the historian's agenda, while to the social scientist concerned with the less developed countries today the problems of agrarian change are of equal significance. Even though the topic still does not command a due share of all historical or social science inquiry, it has already become the focus of a very large literature.

The essays in this book are concerned with historical examples of change within particular agricultural systems and their implications for national economic development. They treat, almost entirely, the period before 1914 and they discuss episodes in the lengthy evolution of the 'western model'. No such small collection of essays on diverse periods and countries can of course purport to constitute either a potted agricultural history of the world or a comprehensive analysis of the connections between agricultural change and the historical performance of whole societies. So much of the world's population has engaged in farming throughout so much of human history, and so much is still so engaged, that the vicissitudes and attainments of agriculture, while rightly claiming an immensely significant place in history, present almost immeasurable problems of description. Much of the hard slog of research on the agrarian past remains to be done. Moreover, the process of economic development forms part and parcel of pervasive societal changes of which the prime causes are not self-evident: it is increasingly recognized that there are no *a priori* reasons why study should be restricted to narrowly 'economic' variables or the techniques associated with particular schools of economic thought. Indeed, these essays illustrate the importance of 'non-economic' variables in the processes of change. The most reasonable approach to the study of development at the present stage of knowledge is that inherent in the aphorism, 'let a hundred flowers bloom'.[1] The widest range of inquiry is enjoined on us and we shall be long about it.

It was with this aim of encouraging more flexible exchanges between historians, social scientists and agriculturists within the University of Reading, which has a large Agriculture Faculty and special overseas service commitments, that the seminar from which this book springs was organized. We were appreciative of the degree of historical scholarship and breadth of view in the contributions secured. In publishing them now, we believe that they will be of more general interest because they discuss a number of major themes in the context of sufficient countries and periods to stimulate suggestive and fruitful comparisons. Our hope is that they may convince some other historians that the opportunities and scope of the field are considerable, and some students of development that the scholarly standards and potential interest of agricultural history can both be high.

There is still much diffidence on the part of students of economic development towards the contribution of agricultural history. Since a *raison d'être* of the seminar and this volume is our conviction that history, carefully and imaginatively written, has something to add to the perspective of their investigation, it is not out of place to look briefly into the reasons for this diffidence. Economic growth is a fashionable theme, and like all such concepts its role in historical writing may finally be judged inadequate or transient. Nevertheless, when historians have turned to economic matters they have – consciously or unconsciously – always been describing processes of growth, failed efforts at growth or obstacles to growth which have at least a family resemblance to modern experience. Not all historians, however, as yet couch their work in forms which are attractive to the eyes of pattern-seeking social scientists. Much historical knowledge which might otherwise be profitably fitted into their 'world view' must appear flimsily based and conceptually weak to students of development. The slenderness of the evidence on which conclusions are sometimes poised cannot, however, be called specifically an historian's failing. It arises from a frequently unavoidable sparseness of quantitative evidence; this pre-statistical phase comes close to the present in the less-developed countries and economists themselves are frequently and necessarily concerned with it. The historian's data problems are not unique.

[1] Quoted by Henry Rosovsky in discussing Rondo Cameron, 'Some Lessons of History for Developing Nations', *American Economic Review*, LVII (1967) p. 334.

Complaint about the analytical poverty of the work of the unspecialized historian has more force. To some extent it may be countered with the argument that the substance, if not the form, of historical writing may still be of interest to the non-historian. But the historical literature is so sprawling and uneven that it clearly requires too much effort for non-historians to locate and mine the paydirt. The result is too often either a rejection of the historical approach by development economists or their dispatch, willy-nilly, to the shelf of standard histories. Unhappily, the tide of research in the journals is now flowing too rapidly past the marker posts of the textbooks for this latter course to be safe.

The standard history books are likely to encourage the belief that the developed countries moved sharply, over some rather brief period of the past, from supposedly static or low-level equilibrium rural conditions to ones of sustained progress. This is reassuring to men troubled by the present difficulties of the less-developed world, as is witnessed by the historical prologues affixed to their work. A single example is sufficient for our purpose: it has very recently been asserted that 'during the half century which followed 1880, Japanese agriculture succeeded in escaping from the stagnation prevalent in monsoon Asia and sustained remarkable growth. . . . The whole process provides a textbook example of how nations with similar climatic and economic conditions might develop.'[1] This statement illustrates a whole school of opinion (though hopefully a dwindling one) that Japan's development was late and abrupt, and that her earlier Tokugawa history was perhaps helpful but by no means decisive for the success of her thrust forward after the Meiji restoration of 1868.[2] We cite the statement not for the sake of mere scholarly dissent but because of its implication that Japan's achievement can readily be repeated elsewhere in Asia. When Japan's centuries of preparation in the form of remarkably 'western-style' commercialization of agriculture are recalled,[3] the parallel drawn with other Asian countries is seen to be not only spurious but capable of leading from false historical premise to tragic contemporary frustration.

[1] Hayami Yujiro, 'Innovations in the Fertilizer Industry and Agricultural Development: the Japanese Experience', *Journal of Farm Economics*, 49 (1967) p. 403.
[2] See especially the views of Henry Rosovsky, 'Japan's transition to Modern Economic Growth, 1868–1885', in H. Rosovsky (ed.), *Industrialization in Two Systems* (New York, 1966) pp. 91–2.
[3] Cf. T. C. Smith, *The Agrarian Origins of Modern Japan* (Stanford, Cal., 1959).

Economic historians of the developed countries are beginning to retreat from their earlier belief in obligingly radical and rapid advances in the past, advances conveniently engineered by an onslaught on some key sector of the economy. One may quote Professor W. A. Cole on England: 'this process of slow growth was the result of a wide, if weak, response to a large number of sectoral growth points, rather than of the stimulus derived from a leading sector';[1] Professor Ross M. Robertson on the United States: 'I am disposed to think, however, that further inquiry into colonial rates of growth may lead to the conclusion that the American economy grew at approximately the same rate for three hundred years';[2] while even Professor Henry Rosovsky has come to accept that agriculture in Japan was substantially more productive at the start of the Meiji era than he had previously believed.[3] But because the debate about new interpretations takes place in numerous specialist journals, the non-specialist is hard put to keep up with it.

Our concern, in the seminar as in this volume, has been to try to narrow the communication gap. In our introduction we have not attempted to distil from the contributions, or from history as a whole, summary messages for development programmes. This, we hope we have made clear, would be premature. Nor, in any case, do we believe that historical experience is likely to offer any single policy prescription. What it can offer is suggestive analogies to modern processes of development. We believe that the essays printed here are pertinent examples of historical scholarship for development economists to read and good ones with which to advertise the subject still further to historians.

The seminar which was the origin of this book was held at the University of Reading in the Lent term 1968. The purpose of the seminar was not a comprehensive survey of the historical instances of agricultural change – an impossible task – but an examination of major problems inherent in the study of the past relationship between agrarian change and economic development. The essays now collected together are based on the papers read to the seminar. The only additions to these papers are Dr Elliott's and Mr Collins's essays, which were specially commissioned by the editors. It has unfortunately proved impossible to include one of the seminar papers, by Dr K. M. Drake on 'Population growth and agricultural change: the Norwegian case, 1800–1850', as it had already been pledged to Dr Wrigley's forthcoming symposium on

[1] *Economic Journal*, LXXVIII (1968) p. 466.
[2] *American Economic Review*, LVII (1967) p. 311.
[3] *Journal of Asian Studies*, XXVII (1968) pp. 347–60.

Agrarian Societies and Population Change. It also proved impossible for Professor Paul David's contribution to the seminar, 'Mechanization in nineteenth-century agriculture – Britain and America', and for Professor Hugh Thomas's paper on 'The sugar trade in Cuba in the eighteenth century' to be included in this volume. Professor R. P. Dore's paper on 'Agricultural improvement in Japan 1870–1900', reprinted here, has previously been published in *Economic Development and Cultural Change,* IX (1960).

Institute of Agricultural History and
Centre for the Advanced Study of Italian Society,
University of Reading

INTRODUCTION: *The historical role of agrarian change in economic development*

I

One of the less palatable lessons of history is that technically advanced and physically productive agricultures do not inevitably bring about a sustained growth of *per capita* real income, much less promote industrialization. The civilizations of Antiquity, with their elaborate agricultures, provide a starting-point. None of them, in the Middle East, Rome, China, Meso-America, in either prehistoric or early historic times, led on to an industrial economy. Technically their farming organization was superb, especially in the wet-rice areas where extensive irrigation networks were dug by *corvées* so large and well drilled as to make the problems of labour management in the early factory system look trifling. Equally, the physical volume of grain they produced was impressive. Yet their social histories are appalling tales of population cycles without a lasting rise in real incomes for the mass of the people on either the upswings or the downswings. Their political histories are cycles of Cathay, the sagas of dynasty after dynasty interrupted only by conquests or palace revolutions which resulted in the replacement of one ruling clique by another. Why were the histories of these early agrarian empires essentially so sterile?

The common feature, notably of the empires with irrigated agricultures, was the immense power of a state apparatus based on a bureaucracy concerned with defence against external threat and the internal maintenance of its own position. Taking a grand view of history, it would be fair to conclude that these bureaucracies aimed at, and succeeded in maintaining, vast peasant societies through long ages and at all population densities in a state of virtual homeostasis. Their great agricultural works, which ensured the addition of new cultivable land by the construction of irrigation canals, extended but did not fundamentally alter the system. Defence, a major commitment of these societies, also often led to vast public works. The outstanding examples are the walled frontiers of China, culminating in the Great Wall, 24 feet high, studded

I

by watchtowers 500 yards apart at the most, and so long that if built in Europe it would enclose large parts of France, Italy, Austria, Switzerland, Hungary, Rumania, Bulgaria, Poland and a segment of Russia.[1] Enormous resources of surveying and engineering skills, construction materials, labour and food (brought up for the workforce from riverine China) were expended on this and other defensive works. Alongside this huge expenditure of energy, the bureaucratic empires were concerned to glorify their rulers in a visible manner by the construction of palaces and tombs, such as the Pyramids. The obligations of the mass of the people, the agricultural peasantry, were to pay taxes and provide labour for the public works. In terms of the diffusion of real wealth these were, of course, crushing obligations.

However impressive their archaeological debris, it is not surprising that these systems did not break through to commercialism or industrialization. The chances that the peasantry might raise their own standard of living significantly and thus provide a broadly based market were severely circumscribed. Tax burdens were so onerous and collection was (all-considered) so efficient that local consumption was kept at a low, often a subsistence level, and might be further depressed in times of stress. Any significant rise in the surplus of food produced above the subsistence level could be skimmed off by the State. Consumer goods of any variety were inevitably only available as luxury items; insufficient income rested in peasant hands to alter this. On the other hand, labour for food production on the family holding and to meet obligations to the State was a real asset. Probably it was this situation which encouraged population growth to meet whatever level of food supplies could be produced and retained by the bulk of the people. Even momentous agricultural advances which might have raised *per capita* real incomes – such as the medieval introduction of early ripening rice or the sixteenth-century introduction of crops like the potato to China[2] – were substantially, though not wholly, neutralized by the responsive growth of population. This response of 'static expansion' – whereby the agricultural base came to support more people without an increase in income per head – was the common historical experience of the pre-industrial world.

The agriculture of much of the under-developed world today is far less impressive technically than were the irrigated systems of Antiquity.

[1] Leonard Cottrell, *The Tiger of Ch'in* (London, 1964) p. 131.
[2] Ping-ti Ho, 'Early Ripening Rice in Chinese History', *Economic History Review*, IX (1956–7) p. 200.

2

Dry-farming does not lend itself to a comparable scale of output. For instance, in the shifting agriculture which is practised (under a whole family of culture names) throughout the tropics, the opportunities of raising production by shortening the period of bush fallow are strictly limited: much of the land must always be left so that the soil may recoup its fertility under secondary vegetation. Neither is output per head likely to be much increased by extending the cultivated zone, for this is more usually a response to population pressure resulting in 'static expansion', and in any case suitable reserves of land are nowadays very scarce. Even if the backward agricultures of the world were to be made as productive as the ancient hydraulic systems, it would be fallacious to assume that economic growth (i.e. rising real incomes per head) or industrialization would follow. Poverty may, perversely, be worsened by the ability of modern medicine to cut the death-rate in countries which remain incapable of raising their product faster than their population can breed. Thus even if food-supply problems are solved and famine averted, the experience of the pre-industrial world, and primitive agricultures even today, would seem to suggest a sharp rise to a new population level, while incomes revert nearly to the previous level.[1] This vicious circle can only be prised open by the conversion of the agricultural surplus into a rising effective demand for non-agricultural commodities – other than children!

It was this which even the impressively organized empires of Antiquity could not achieve. High peasant demand was rendered inconceivable by the very nature of the systems. Nor could these empires produce a sizeable alternative demand from non-peasant (professional or commercial) classes, capable of calling forth manufactured wares from more than local, craftsmen sources. The division of labour, and the diffusion of artisan skills, is limited by the extent of the market. The market for basic manufactured goods in these societies (as in all primitive and poor agrarian societies) was so small as to cramp the possibilities for the division of manufacturing labour and the consequent emergence of an appreciable class of technicians, who would themselves add to the market. Small wonder that sixteenth-century Chinese and Indian rulers

[1] E.g. the increases in prehistoric Central American populations with successive agricultural improvements; or the rapid expansion and southward movement of Negro populations in East Africa in the sixteenth century, based on the introduction of new food plants like taro as a result of Moslem trade with India (R. S. MacNeish, 'The Origins of New World Civilization', *Scientific American*, 211 (1964) pp. 29–37; C. S. Coon, *The History of Man* (Harmondsworth: Pelican Books, 1967) p. 335).

3

sought European gunfounders as eagerly as they sought European cannon.[1] The bureaucratic empires were organized to attain a large total product from agriculture and to ensure security against outside attack. Such a social order, with a small and self-regarding central authority, was prone to squander resources on sterile religious and funerary monuments, and to permit or even encourage population growth up to whatever levels of food production could be reached. This is not to say that these societies endured the static technology or static equilibria which economists are prone to hypothesize as the historical condition: as we have seen, there were from time to time technological advances, notably with the post-Columbian dispersal of higher-yielding food plants; equally there were repeated population crashes of horrifying dimensions. But since population densities tended to catch up rapidly with any new level of output, the fundamental constraints of the socio-economic system remained.

Even when highly productive agricultural systems developed in the far more flexible societies of medieval Europe they did not carry the economies through to industrialization, as Professor Zangheri shows below in his discussion of the early history of Lombardy and as Professor Slicher van Bath shows in his examination of the islands of intensive agriculture which appeared only a little later around several western European cities.[2] What seemed to be needed was an increase of productivity over a wide market area; a breathing space from intense population pressure during which income rather than men might be multiplied; and a sufficiently wide distribution of this rise in income to generate demand not simply for the hand-carving of a few luxury items, but for the large-scale production of standardized and simple commodities. Historically the fulfilment of these conditions has been very rare.

II

When the constellation did emerge it was immensely potent. It appeared in England, parts of western Europe, North America and Japan in

[1] C. M. Cipolla, *Guns and Sails in the Early Phase of European Expansion 1400–1700* (London, 1965) p. 111.

[2] B. H. Slicher van Bath, 'The Rise of Intensive Husbandry in the Low Countries', in J. S. Bromley and E. H. Kossman (eds.), *Britain and the Netherlands* (London, 1960) p. 147. This is also true of Poland and eastern Europe, which increased agricultural production markedly in the sixteenth and seventeenth centuries: M. Malowist, 'The problem of the inequality of economic development in Europe in the later Middle Ages', *Econ. Hist. Rev.*, 2nd ser., XIX (1966) pp. 15–28.

4

periods ranging from the mid-seventeenth to the mid-nineteenth centuries.[1] This was a short episode of world history but laden with significance for the future. The constellation appeared in relatively few countries, ones which were favoured in that they were climatically temperate and generally well endowed with the indented coastlines and river networks which alone at that time made possible the long-distance transport of cereals. These were decided advantages, without which it is difficult to imagine these countries developing their economies so rapidly. But they were advantages which were activated only in special historical circumstances and it is these we need to identify. To do so we must invoke three strands of history, the demographic, sociological and agricultural, even though it would be arbitrary to treat them as separate or independent variables, so complex was their interaction.

In all the countries where industrialization took place early, population pressure in the immediately preceding period had dropped, both because of a fall in the rate of population growth (or an actual decrease of population) and because agricultural output increased more rapidly.[2] This is not the place for a discussion of how far the slower rate of population growth was separate from, or linked with, concurrent changes in agricultural productivity and market opportunities. It is enough to observe the crucial significance of a demographic lull for the development of industrialism.

In the same societies a new class of farmers emerged. Western European societies, of which North America was in the main a transplanted version, were polycentric, with fragmented sources of authority and initiative. Within their agricultures, particularly in the Low Countries and England, independent and market-oriented farmers had been able to arise out of the breakdown of communal farming in the depression of the late Middle Ages. In western Europe areas reclaimed and settled late were similarly characterized by separate farms occupied by independent producers. There was thus scope for considerable diversity of economic action and response. The uneven endowment of soil types made it possible, sometimes even necessary, to exchange food of different kinds between different districts. Regional exchanges of certain agricultural products – cereals, livestock and wool – developed

[1] See E. L. Jones, 'Agricultural Origins of Industry', *Past and Present*, 40 (1968) pp. 58–71, and 'Le origini agricole dell'industria', *Studi Storici*, IX (1968) pp. 564–93.
[2] K. F. Helleiner, 'The Population of Europe from the Black Death to the eve of the Vital Revolution', in E. E. Rich and C. H. Wilson (eds.), *The Cambridge Economic History of Europe*, IV (Cambridge, 1967) pp. 58–94.

B

merchanting institutions in medieval times and made possible a moderate growth of towns, whose burghers grew less and less of their own food. The more fertile areas showed their capacity to raise the overall supply of food, and their ability to supply the whole community offered the less fertile spots both scope and incentive to produce non-agricultural goods for exchange.

In both town and country in western Europe there arose what is generically if somewhat misleadingly called a 'middle class', consisting of commercial and industrial groups and independent farmers. The development of these groups to sizeable and ultimately dominant levels was crucial to the expansion of the market and the emergence of entrepreneurs, agricultural and industrial, to supply it. This chapter of sociological history is involved and controversial, but for our purposes it is almost enough that there was such a history. The independent, commercial elements which emerged between the peasantry at one end of the social scale and the ruling lords, lay and ecclesiastic, and their officials at the other end, expanded in Europe as it had done nowhere else. It was an effect of incipient economic development and a cause of each further step in that direction, stimulating a market for wares below the luxury class and ensuring a supply of owner-managers who had a peculiar interest in efficient production for the market. All too little is known about the origins of these taste-leaders and how they overcame traditional and cultural resistance to innovation in both agriculture and industry, but the existence and importance of such a spearhead is clear.[1]

Farming for the market reached unprecedented heights of intensity around the textile towns of late medieval Flanders. These towns represented the largest concentration of manufacturing in northern Europe, initially working wool from England and elsewhere into cloth for parts of Germany, which in return exported cereals. The agriculture surrounding these towns was directed towards producing industrial crops – flax, madder and hops – and towards the intensive feeding of livestock, for which clover was sown as early as the fourteenth century. Intensive irrigated agriculture had developed even earlier to feed the cloth towns of northern Italy. But one crucial difference between the two areas was to be found in the capacity of Flemish and Brabanter rotations to support mixed farming on thin soils and dry uplands, and so to transform the agricultures of north-west Europe. Even so, it took centuries

[1] Professor Dore's contribution below discusses a later phase of the activities of such a stratum in Japan.

6

of adaptation and experiment to gain acceptance for working systems involving forage crops *and* cereals; indeed, the Flemish farmers themselves often bought rather than grew cereals, so specialized had they become.

The strategic innovations in Flanders – subsequently transferred to England – involved the growing of forage crops (legumes and roots) in place of fallow, which allowed the raising of herds and flocks on farms without any reduction of the grain acreage – indeed, with an actual increase of grain yields resulting from the increased production of organic manure. Information about this possibility spread slowly. In England, the first country to take advantage of them, the new fodder crops were merged to produce mixed farming systems from about 1630. Although efforts were still being made to reproduce versions of mixed farming on backward claylands in the third quarter of the nineteenth century, it seems that the initial uptake on suitable soils was already sufficient for production to run a little ahead of demand by the late seventeenth century. Mixed farming went from strength to strength during the eighteenth century. It became involved with radical changes in the structure of landholdings. Those parts of England which clung to co-operative farming and its archaic regulations (which may have reduced risk and offered fair shares but did not produce much to share) were increasingly assimilated to the developing sectors. In the exceptional wartime food crisis of 1800–1 Sir Joseph Banks wrote to an unnamed peer pressing for a temporary Act of Parliament to encourage potato planting on the fallows and observed that fallowing in the unenclosed parishes was a 'customary mode of Culture, derived from remote antiquity'. But he was obliged to admit that it had been given up elsewhere: 'in light soils especially it appears to be universally allowed, that Arable will continue in an unimpaired state if not in a progressive course of improvement, provided it regularly receives from the Cultivator the whole of the Manure produced upon it'.[1] In England the improvements had not initially required legal licence in the form of enclosure Acts; they had often been introduced by private action or semi-formal agreements. By the mid-eighteenth century the new systems had already raised agricultural productivity in England quite considerably and parliamentary enclosure had to be invoked thereafter merely to generalize a process which was well under way.

Outside the Low Countries, continental western Europe was slower

[1] Board of Agriculture, Early MSS. Rothamsted Experimental Station: Letter from Sir Joseph Banks, 3.ii.1801.

to change. The diffusion of agricultural innovations had affected only a small part of northern France before about 1770, and it needed the pressure of population and the Napoleonic assault on tenurial systems in France and western Germany to speed up the process. However, well before such an acceleration, parts of north-western, central and southern Europe were in receipt of cheap grain from east of the Elbe, where serfdom was being reimposed. Only in the crowded, eroded lands of Mediterranean Europe (and until 1750, France) was food in seriously short supply.

North America presented a basically similar appearance to north-west Europe: ample food production (due to the extension of the cultivated area, as well as to improved methods), accompanied by regional differences in factor endowments which generated specialization and trade in agricultural products. By the mid-eighteenth century, in fact, a dynamic was beginning to appear on the side of agricultural supply which foreshadowed the later problems of over-production in the agricultures of the western world and its overseas suppliers; indeed, the problem of over-production emerged in an export crop, Virginian tobacco, very early in the seventeenth century and was countered by an effort to maintain prices through the enforced burning of part of the crop.[1]

In this briefest of sketches of the spearhead of early developing countries, no mention has so far been made of Japan, which to western students appears as the odd man out. It is worth establishing the general correspondence between Japanese and European patterns of early modern development. The Tokugawa shoguns brought internal peace and a unification of the national market to Japan early in the seventeenth century, and under their dynasty the Japanese economy advanced adequately to support a large urban population, much internal trade in agricultural products, and a vigorous spread of cottage industry, with all the growth of a mercantile community which this implies. It is true that the Meiji flowering of industry in Japan lagged behind that of Britain, parts of Europe, and the United States, and that it borrowed from these countries; but on the time-scale of history this lag was slight – much less evident than the continuing failure of the rest of Asia to follow. The earlier productivity increases in Japan and the changes in the nature of the society which they had made possible in Tokugawa times were surely crucial to Japan's achievement.

Early in the Tokugawa period there was a transition from holdings

---

[1] J. K. Galbraith, *American Capitalism* (Harmondsworth: Pelican Books, 1963), pp. 169–70.

with large numbers of subordinate labourers, the *genin*, to small farms founded on the nuclear family unit. It must be presumed that there was a net gain from this wider spread of managerial-entrepreneurial opportunities and incentives. We know that the provincial lords became interested in improving agriculture to cater for the towns, part of whose growth was politically inspired. New techniques of farming were introduced which are in part strikingly reminiscent of those which have latterly been identified as critical ones in England. The innovations were individually small and comparatively cheap and thus, as in England, were suitable for wide diffusion among a large number of operators. Accounts of innovation in Tokugawa agriculture and in seventeenth-century English farming may be compared. T. C. Smith writes of Japan, 'innovations rarely if ever came singly, they hung together in clusters by a kind of inner logic; one innovation brought others in its train, and often could not be adopted independently of them'; M. A. Havinden writes of England, 'there was an ascending spiral of progress . . . each advance, while small in itself, stimulated further advance in another sector, and the spiral was able to begin again at a higher level'.[1] The Japanese innovations included row cultivation, more and better-selected plant varieties, new crops like sweet potatoes, peanuts and some vegetables, and the increased use of iron implements, treadmills and pumps for irrigation. The English innovations began with the sowing of grass leys on the fallows, permitting the raising of more livestock which in turn necessitated the sowing of new and valuable fodder crops like sainfoin and clover to provide winter feed. The result, in Japan as in England, was a release of resources from the agricultural sector into the economy as a whole. In both countries the socio-economic system permitted the increase in real wealth to be put to use in what proved to be preparation for an industrial society. The increase in food supplies in Japan, as in north-west Europe, was not eaten away by a commensurate growth of population: between 1720 and 1840 there was only a very slow growth of population. The degree of urbanization attained in earlier Tokugawa times was almost maintained. Independent farming, inter-regional trade and urbanization increased productivity in eighteenth-century Japan in ways which were fundamentally similar to those of the other advanced countries and certainly very different from the experience of Africa or mainland Asia.

[1] T. C. Smith, *The Agrarian Origins of Modern Japan* (Stanford, Cal., 1959) p. 101; M. A. Havinden, 'Agricultural Progress in Openfield Oxfordshire', *Agricultural History Review*, IX (1961) p. 83.

III

What was the essence of the innovations and what was the scale of increases in productivity? The husbandry improvements which we have referred to were of a distinctive cast. They were biological and organizational. They were widely diffused and mutually propulsive amendments to rotations, which tended to eliminate fallow and certainly increased the supply of organic manure. They involved the remoulding of systems of farm management into more productive systems of mixed farming. They were associated with advances in seed selection and animal breeding.

This first wave of improvements was followed in the nineteenth century by a second wave, consisting of better hand-tool technologies (releasing labour from agriculture as the first wave had not) and heavy applications of artificial fertilizer which greatly raised crop yields. This wave overlapped the first, and it affected the advanced countries within a much shorter period, presumably because once small industrial bases had been established they could supply the metallurgical and chemical inputs which characterized the second wave.

The second wave – the 'proto-industrial' phase of agricultural advance – was thus distinguished firstly by the adoption of the scythe in place of the sickle in the grain harvest. The corn scythe reduced the labour needed to take the harvest, even though yields were rising as a result of the contemporaneous increase in fertilizer applications. Possibly the scythe had been used for harvesting cereals in tenth-century Lombardy; certainly it was used for cereals in the Low Countries of the fifteenth century. The explosive phase of its spread came, however, in England, western Europe and Scandinavia from the end of the eighteenth century; the cradle scythe was adopted in North America in the nineteenth century; while the corn scythe spread into central and eastern Europe in the nineteenth and twentieth centuries, and into parts of southern Europe and the Middle East during the twentieth century.[1] The second distinctive mark of the proto-industrial wave was the great increase in the use of artificial fertilizers. Inputs of these rose in a very steep curve in nineteenth-century Britain. As superphosphate came in there was a powerful feedback to the industrial sector in the form of an expansion of heavy chemical plants to meet the demand for sulphuric acid. Crop yields rose substantially.

[1] E. J. T. Collins, 'Labour supply and demand in European agriculture, 1800–1880', discusses aspects of this below.

Similar movements were evident only a little later in all the advanced countries. In France, for instance, the first, biological wave of agricultural changes apparently followed an enclosure movement more directly, and was compressed into a narrower time span. The adoption of the potato between 1740 and 1770 ended the periodic French famines; clover and other fodder crops, and maize, came in between 1770 and 1790; sugar beet grown for sugar and for pulp to feed livestock came in under the continental system. This wave therefore included cleaning crops and forage crops which helped to suppress the fallow while facilitating the feeding of stock on arable farms: that is, it produced mixed farming. The wave seems to have lost its momentum in the second quarter of the nineteenth century, while the proto-industrial wave quickly succeeded it during the third quarter. Heavy fertilizer and lime application from 1850 to 1880 followed the construction of a railway network, and produced a rise of 50 per cent in wheat yields between those dates. The fundamental, if unspectacular, adoption of the scythe was likewise a feature of the Second Empire.[1]

It has been calculated (for England and Japan) that the first wave of change approximately doubled the medieval yields of food crops; and that the second wave (stretching in the case of fertilizers to the present) has doubled yields again, 50 per cent of this second jump being attributable to the direct effects of chemical fertilizers.[2] Professor Thompson has observed of the proto-industrial phase in England, however, that whereas approximately half the farmland and half the farm output came under a system which involved farmers in purchasing raw materials in the cheapest market and processing them in their farm businesses 'just like any cotton lord',[3] undoubtedly fewer than half the farm operators were involved. The diffusion of innovation has a logic of its own in all systems where spontaneous adoption and free communication and emulation among farmers are permitted.[4] The advanced countries with which we have been dealing had long been 'prepared' by the earlier commercialization of large sections of their agricultures for a system in which more and more of their farmers would come, in the second wave,

[1] C. P. Kindleberger, *Economic Growth in France and Britain 1851–1950* (Cambridge, Mass., 1964) pp. 211–13.

[2] H. L. Richardson, 'What Fertilizers Could Do to Increase World Food Production', *Advancement of Science*, XVII (1961) p. 479.

[3] F. M. L. Thompson, 'The Second Agricultural Revolution, 1815–1880', *Econ. Hist. Rev.*, 2nd ser., XXI (1968) p. 71.

[4] G. E. Jones, 'The Adoption and Diffusion of Agricultural Practices', *World Agricultural Economy and Rural Sociology Abstr.*, 9 (1967).

to purchase and process inputs. Nevertheless, it must be emphasized that fewer than half the farmers, even in nineteenth-century England, really participated in the second wave.

It is unfortunately not self-evident that anything like as many 'deviant' individuals exist in the under-developed world to generate comparably swift innovation.[1] If only a sufficient number did exist, there might be a telescoping of the first and second waves by building – primarily – fertilizer plants in the under-developed world. This has been done, of course, in countries like India, but the slowness with which farmers have come forward to use the simple and cheap inputs made available to them has disappointed those who expected a reflex response to the profit motive. There appear to be severe blockages created by the risks and costs involved in destabilizing the bio-economic systems which even primitive farming constitutes.[2] These risks are translated into cultural disapprobation of novelty in its critical inception period. The individualistic systems of the developed countries in early modern times permitted rather more freedom of action to those who perceived the prospects for change.

IV

Although so far we have not discussed directly the influence of these agricultural developments on industrialization, we have assumed that in the early developed countries such an influence existed. The numerous small rotational changes of the first, biological, wave of change were certainly suitable for extension among successive generations of farmers in the developed countries. Even there, changes in the ownership and occupation of the land had sometimes to be forced through to speed the process, although it should be questioned to what extent such changes in agrarian structure were engineered simply as transfers of land resources into more powerful hands at times when farming was very profitable.

The first wave of change made it possible for the developed countries to cope with the dramatic rise in population which, in Europe, began in the mid-eighteenth century. With a great deal of activity and alarm, and

[1] For an exhaustive discussion of these obstacles to agricultural change in the less-developed countries, in particular India, see Gunnar Myrdal, *Asian Drama*, II (London, 1968).

[2] Some of the problems involved in transformations as drastic as these are discussed by Dr Elliott in his contribution below.

12

by using overseas territories as both dumping grounds for population and sources of food for the home countries, Europe slipped past the Malthusian trap.

The rise in *per capita* agricultural output which had begun earlier meant not merely that the population could grow but that more of it could move into the towns. It also produced a situation of internal competition within the developing agricultures which drove more and more small farmers, or their landless sons, in those areas which were poor for farming to look for something else to sell. Gradually farmhouse and cottage manufacturing thickened in the less fertile districts. The period 1650–1750 in Europe and the period 1750–1850 in North America and Japan experienced these changes, which produced three outstanding effects. First, the agricultural populations of the more fertile regions were able to acquire (and develop tastes for) purchased manufactured wares in return for their surplus foodstuffs. Second, the group of putting-out merchants employing the occupants of cottages and small farms in domestic manufacturing expanded considerably and gained business skill in the process. Third, a sizeable proportion of what would otherwise have been a peasantry with no expertise outside agriculture came to possess some of the skills and habits of a manufacturing population. Much agricultural history has dealt with the scale of the outflow of labour from agriculture and too little with its real suitability for manufacturing industry. There was a point beyond which the ratio of common labourers to artisans and machine operatives could not rise, and the likelihood is that a fieldhand newly arrived in town would be fit only for common labouring. Significantly, in mid-nineteenth-century England Edwin Chadwick was told by a firm which hired out steam-engines that they were willing to have them handled only by their own staff, 'for they cannot trust their engines in such hands as are at present to be got amongst farm servants'.[1] But someone accustomed to cottage industry was much more suitable as a recruit to the factory age. Apart from these particular effects, the large size of agriculture and its process-ing and servicing industries until a very late date, together with the reliance of many more manufacturing processes than nowadays on agricultural raw materials, meant that agriculture's influence on econo-mic development was very great. Its details constitute a most complex maze of interactions.[2]

[1] Edwin Chadwick, 'The Demand for more Intelligent Labour in Agricul-ture', *Journ. Stat. Soc.*, XXVII (1865) p. 32.
[2] Professor Thompson's contribution below deals with a major aspect of this interaction.

We have laid heavy stress on the economic significance of agricultural innovation, which carries with it the assumption that a significant increase in agricultural output necessarily precedes, or accompanies, industrialization. The case against such emphasis – that agricultural expansion beyond the subsistence level is a consequence rather than a cause of economic development – has been made by some economists, most directly by Professor Neumark.[1] Neumark's thesis is based on a model of a two-sector closed economy (i.e. with negligible levels of agricultural or industrial exports), within which the peasants cannot buy manufactured goods because they do not produce a surplus for sale and manufacturers hardly produce at all because there is too little food on sale to sustain an industrial workforce. To introduce agricultural innovation as the dynamic element in such an economy is erroneous, according to Neumark, because it fails to explain 'why the peasants should want to expand their production in the first place'. What must first appear is a market, which Neumark finds in overseas demand. As an example he instances Japan. Here, he claims, there is 'no historical foundation' for thinking agricultural productivity rose ahead of, rather than responded to, industrial development; the engine of growth was an export trade in raw silk and rice which began with the start of the Meiji era. The difficulty about such an argument is that it presupposes that those countries which *imported* food were already sufficiently advanced to produce the ready cash to pay for it. Professor Neumark, in fact, has exported to them the problem of origins. It is, in reality, difficult to conceive of a big urban-industrial growth ahead of an increasing output from agriculture. An obligatory pre-condition for the continuous expansion of cities and a specialist industrial workforce must be a food surplus; however small a percentage of the total crop this surplus represented, it had to be present and it had to be reliable.

Where the early stages of economic development were as lengthy and gradual as in the developed countries the search for a decisive initial impetus to growth from a single sector is artificial, even as an heuristic device. Yet it does seem possible to discern that, over two or three generations, the first wave of agricultural change released a large flow of resources into the economy. In the English case a larger agricultural output apparently did not automatically turn itself off – by reducing prices and forcing marginal farmers out of production – because there existed sharp distinctions within agriculture which gave rise to internal

[1] S. D. Neumark, *Foreign Trade and Economic Development in Africa: A Historical Perspective* (Stanford, Cal., 1964) pp. 192–6.

14

competition, and hence the success of some groups of farmers even during periods of general difficulty.[1]

Resources were transferred from English agriculture in a variety of ways: better food supplies permitted a continuation of population growth, held down purchases of overseas food at rather low levels, and kept the subsistence wage of labour low. Raw materials were supplied to industry at an acceptable price. Capital may have been released, although this is unclear – its clearest aspect is agriculture's contribution to the building of the communications network. This was crucially important to industrialists, but agriculturists were prepared to invest disproportionately in its creation because of their dispersed locations and need to collect and transport bulky goods to market. Labour was probably not released from agriculture during the first wave of change – mixed farming had heavy labour needs and the absolute number of farmhands actually grew – but the nation's food supply could be secured by an ever smaller *proportion* of the national workforce. Markets for manufactured goods were provided by agriculture: consumer goods were purchased by its prosperous sections even at times of low prices, since farmers constituted a solid section of that middle-class market whose demand was of such importance; producer goods were always absorbed because even the first wave of agricultural change made increasing demands on non-farm inputs.[2] The second wave of change, building on the small industrial sector to which the first wave had so greatly contributed, placed heavier demands on industry for ever more powerful inputs, so that a self-reinforcing interaction between agriculture and industry continued.

The complex flows of resources in England's economic development would appear to have been mirrored in western Europe, the European offshoots in North America and Australasia, and in Japan. But the success of this development transformed the conditions which had made it possible, and increased the difficulties of 'late-comers'. A flood of farm products from the extra-European territories tumbled prices in the last quarter of the nineteenth century. Agricultural progress had been too successful for its own good, both within Europe and overseas. The first flush of economic success in western Europe had been the historically

[1] See E. L. Jones, 'Agriculture and Economic Growth in England, 1660–1750: Agricultural Change', reprinted in his *Agriculture and Economic Growth in England, 1650–1815* (London, 1967).

[2] For a recent attempt to demonstrate the importance of eighteenth-century agricultural development in England and France for the growth of the iron industry, see Paul Bairoch, 'Le Rôle de l'Agriculture dans la Création de la Sidérurgie Moderne', *Revue d'Histoire Économique et Sociale*, fasc. 1 (1966) pp. 5–23.

unprecedented reaction of agricultural innovation in a fluid socio-economic matrix. It had helped the 'early-comers' to industrialize rapidly. For the under-developed countries there could and can be no hope of emulating such slow and special economic chemistry: the threshold needs of industrial investment had changed, the parameters of history had budged.

V

The early stages in the economic development of western Europe provoked immediate and long-term repercussions in the outside world. Two frontiers outside Europe were bound up with the emergence of its markets – the plantation frontier of the tropical and sub-tropical world and the frontiers of agriculture in the temperate grasslands. The contrast of their history offers an illuminating example of the effects on economic development of different climatic conditions and social systems. For while the one remained closely tied and subordinate to Europe, the other was able to break away into rapid autochthonous agricultural and industrial growth.

The most obvious function of the plantation frontier was to supply Europe with tropical and semi-tropical crops. In this it was extravagantly successful. Sugar imports to London, for example, were negligible before the Civil War; rose to 148,000 cwt in 1663–9; and 371,000 cwt in 1699–1701, a third of the last figure being re-exported. Similarly the 20,000 lb of tobacco which Virginia and Maryland had sent to England in 1619 had risen to 9 million lb by the 1660s, to 15 million lb by the late 1680s and to 22 million lb by 1700. Two-thirds of the last quantity were re-exported, despite considerable tobacco growing in the Netherlands and Germany.[1] It was this amazing increase of colonial production, as we have already noted in the case of the Virginian tobacco planters, which led at a very early date to the characteristic crises of over-production of primary products subsequently experienced by international trade.

The history of the plantation frontier can best be exemplified by the development of sugar production. The sugar frontier was located early on in the eastern Meditearranean, where Europeans came into contact with the Moslem use of cane. The frontier moved westwards through the Mediterranean during the Middle Ages; it reached the Portuguese Atlantic islands in the fifteenth century; Brazil early in the sixteenth

[1] Ralph Davis, *A Commercial Revolution* (London, 1967) pp. 10–11.

century; from there, when the Portuguese determined to oust them, Dutch sugar growers moved to the West Indies where they taught the British the tricks of the trade. Spaniards had already brought sugar cane to the Caribbean; the French began to show an active interest; and the subsequent history of the West Indies is very much one of struggle for supremacy in sugar production in the context of shifting internal frontiers of cultivation as the heavy demands of cane on the soil exhausted some islands and made it difficult for them to compete against those more recently brought under the crop. British sugar cultivation was eclipsed towards the end of the eighteenth century by French islands and (in the nineteenth century) by Cuba and Puerto Rico, which the Spanish still held.

The Caribbean sugar islands formed one triangulation point in the Atlantic trade of the early industrial period. The trade involved the dispatch of British manufactures to West Africa, in return for slaves taken on to the West Indies, in return for sugar which was exported to Europe and North America. The West Indies also required European manufactures, and because they were so specialized in sugar production as to grow insufficient food for their own needs they required grain from the 'Middle Colonies' of North America and cod from New England, as well as timber and horses to work the sugar mills.

The colonial sugar industry was thus highly organized. It was composed of efficient business units employing slave labour and performing the earlier stages of refining *in situ*, using relatively expensive milling equipment. All kinds of demands were set up for the manufactured products of the home country. 'The colonies', writes Professor Ralph Davis, 'were the destinations of great exports of iron wares and later of cottons which played a vital part in the building of those industries to the point where technical change transformed the momentum of growth.'[1] Significantly, the maritime, colonizing countries took the lead over the land-locked, but metallurgically advanced countries of central Europe. Hajo Holborn has commented that after 1648, 'Germany became for the next 150 years a back-yard of the emerging Atlantic world, a world whose maritime and colonial enterprises created the wealth on which the modern societies of Europe were founded.'[2] The pregnant significance of the combined home and overseas markets which were available to England, the first industrializer, cannot go unremarked.

[1] Ralph Davis, *The Rise of the English Shipping Industry* (London, 1962) p. 393.
[2] H. Holborn, *A History of Modern Germany 1648–1840* (London, 1965) p. 27.

A second frontier, and with it a totally different social system, began to edge across the temperate grasslands of the Americas, South Africa and later Australasia, with the migration and settlement of European farmers and ranchers. North America, Australasia and the livestock frontiers of South Africa and Argentina became substantial sources of food for western Europe. Initially, in exchange, all of them imported European manufactures, but the erosion of this market began early with the breakaway of the United States from Britain, and its creation within two generations of an industrial sector which was in some respects more advanced than the British one. The American settler population, the 'mere earth scratchers' as Gibbon Wakefield called them, was of European origin and was still located in temperate realms. Therefore it possessed European tastes for consumer goods and it could continue to employ a European-type agricultural technology which implied a demand for European producer goods. Unlike the slave-plantation economies of the tropical and southern colonies, the North American population of independent farmers thus offered a large potential market for simple durable goods. We have already indicated that concentrations of rural domestic manufacturers arose in America (in New England) through a similar process of regional specialization to that envisaged for all the advanced countries. From these localities the human material for the industrialization process, labour and management, was recruited. The slaves of plantation agriculture were unable to move into industry until a late date. Similarly, industrial entre-preneurship and investment were not readily forthcoming from plantation societies where opportunity and wealth were so tightly restricted.

The northern states of North America best exemplify how a European-type society presented with enormous scope to expand temperate agriculture could generate its own, very advanced, industries. The development of simple mass-produced goods was of key importance to the process. At its heart lies the mass-production of metal axe-heads, guns and ploughs. Axes, which will serve as an illustration, were the basic requirement for the timber industry and its complementary occupation, clearing land for farming. In any given month for a full half-century there was a demand for 40,000 new axes in North America. The original blacksmith-made axe-heads had to be replaced after only a month of use and resharpening. The entire process was revolutionized by the Collins brothers in Ohio between 1826 and 1832 by the introduction, first, of air-driven forges to rotate the grindstones and then of precision, semi-automated methods of tempering large numbers of axe-heads simultaneously on a drum revolving in a furnace. The uniform mass product had arrived. After the Collins brothers' axes came Samuel Colt's revolver, mass-produced from inter-changeable parts, which was the essence of the 'American system' of manufacturing. As the axe had permitted the assault on the northern woodlands, so the Colt revolver helped the Americans to bring the cattle industry to the western plains, Comanche country. Nor was it an accident that an old Colt employee, Henry Leland, was the first to adapt mass-production techniques to the making of automobiles. The sheer numbers of farm families in the American rural market permitted this distinctive extension of industrialism. The initial interdependence in agricultural and industrial growth was as clear in the temperate zone of North America as in the developed countries of western Europe. Planta-tion agriculture offered no such scope.

VI

The spectacular success of the industrialized countries and their over-seas annexes wholly transformed the historical conditions of economic development. The onrush of their technology has heightened the capital costs of industrialization, raising the barriers facing would-be developing nations. The wealth gap between the developed and the under-developed world is growing.

The industrial countries in most cases needed to import food, but while they were few and rich, there were many poor primary-producing countries. The terms of trade tended to move in favour of manufactured exports; advances in the cultivation of export crops often served only to exacerbate this situation, a situation in which the under-developed world could not amass sufficient capital to set up its own modern industries. The opportunities to ease resources out of agriculture and with the same stroke home-produce some basic consumer durables, using intermediate technologies and village industrialization, receded into the past as one or two prestige factories became capable of meeting cheaply the limited effective demand of poor peoples.

These difficulties faced by the primary-producing countries have been compounded by the inability of the developed countries to contract their agricultures.[1] Cheap imported food in the late nineteenth century put

[1] See M. M. Postan, *An Economic History of Western Europe 1945–1964* (London, 1967), and Gavin McCrone, *The Economics of Subsidising Agriculture* (London, 1962).

19

severe strains on home agricultures, but was countered over much of Europe by the restrictive response of tariff walls: the result was the conservation of large cereal-growing sectors which might otherwise have shrunk appreciably (as they did in the late nineteenth century and the interwar period in England, where there was no such protection). Wars and phases of world food shortages have tended to lead to financial and political support for agriculture which can only be reversed slowly once conditions appear to have improved. These problems are made more troublesome by runaway technological changes still continuing within the sector. Advanced technology tends to be adopted first and most by the richer and better-educated farmers; by raising the supply of already well-filled markets it threatens constantly to reduce prices, and hence pushes the net farm incomes of the many small, less efficient producers below acceptable welfare levels. To maintain these incomes a heavy exchequer burden has to be carried.

The supply price of farmers in the industrial countries is well below the price of comparable businessmen, so that it requires exceptionally severe price pressure on the farm sector to induce producers to leave. Nevertheless, there is a widespread political assumption that all farmers have a right to remain in the industry. Agricultural producers' organizations tend to have political power in the industrial democracies out of all proportion to their real ability to deliver a voting bloc. In consequence, most developed countries provide considerable financial support for agriculture, support related more to agriculture's tenacious hold on political power than to its current economic contribution. The repercussions on the under-developed countries as primary producers are almost unmitigatedly negative.

The problems of the under-developed world are of course far more serious. They are problems less of the rational disposal of ample resources in order to become still richer than of how to dispose of minimal resources in order to cease being unbearably poor. Before all else, output needs to be expanded fast enough to overhaul the rapid growth of population which has been facilitated by medical improvements. But successful agricultural projects, if they accentuate the movement into the towns, may merely shift the location of the fundamental human problem – poverty. Many towns in the poorer countries are shanty towns, and even the better established cities can seldom provide employment, accommodation and public services fast enough to cope with a swollen influx of displaced peasants.[1] Until the population pressure is relieved and the urban alternatives made more attractive developing societies will continue to be faced by a double problem: many of those leaving agriculture will enter abominable town conditions and many of those who remain will clamour for the dismemberment of great land-holdings into tiny, economically inefficient plots.[2]

We are reluctant to conclude so pessimistically, but it is clear that agricultural development is not enough. While a rapid exodus from the countryside may be a heartening sign that the threat of starvation has been met, it may merely represent the transfer of endemic poverty from the rural to the urban sector. Big urban agglomerations of under-employed and discontented humanity pose an obviously greater threat to internal and international stability than do big, dispersed populations of toiling peasants.

[1] Cf. the expressive account of the conversion of 'tribesmen into corner boys' in Baghdad, in Gavin Maxwell, *A Reed Shaken by the Wind* (London, 1959) pp. 13–15.
[2] Professor Carr discusses the history of the latter reaction in Mexico in his contribution below.

1 The historical relationship between agricultural and economic development in Italy

R. ZANGHERI

The theme of this seminar embraces both the study of the past and the analysis of present-day economic problems of developing countries. The obstacles which these countries are facing today are, in certain essential aspects, different in nature from those which were faced and variously overcome by the industrialized countries. In fact, these obstacles are to be found not only within the under-developed economies but also in the relationship which has been created between their economies and the world market.

Nevertheless I would basically agree with those who hold that in all known cases the development of a modern industrial economy has been closely conditioned by the stimuli and resources of agriculture. There is an increasingly widespread belief that an industrial revolution and an agrarian revolution are, in fact, part of a single process. The English model, as I shall point out later, is particularly suited to illustrating a theory of the unity and continuity of modern economic development, not least because it is an almost self-contained case-study, only minimally effected by independent international economic changes. In different conditions of isolation, Soviet industrialization was also closely tied to agrarian transformation. In this case, the dramatic shortening of the period of time in which it took place made the processes of agricultural and industrial change almost simultaneous.

I hardly need to say that it would be misleading to view as the same historical process events so different as the industrial revolution in England, the early Soviet five-year plans, and the so far unfortunately unsuccessful efforts of the newly independent countries to industrialize. In the first example, the generating factor was profit in conditions of a competitive capitalist economy; in the second case, it was the highly centralized direction of a state economy; in the third instance, the direction has oscillated among various stimuli. The historical periods are different, and consequently the necessary conditions for entering the industrial area have changed. The departure points were also different. This is why I regard the assertion that the English industrial revolution was to all intents and purposes a successful attempt by an under-developed economy to reach the point of 'take-off' as a facile simplifica-tion. As has recently been noted, by the middle of the eighteenth century England had already reached 'a higher level of economic development than the more backward countries in the world today'.[1] And, one can add, not least because it utilized the resources of those countries which are today backward. England between 1750 and 1850 was also faced by an international structure of markets which was wholly different from that facing countries like Germany and Italy when they created their in-dustrial base in the late nineteenth and early twentieth centuries – not to speak of countries which have tried to industrialize in more recent periods.

It is clear that Italy – to limit myself to a single example for the purposes of this essay – began to experience a modern industrial trans-formation at a time when profound changes had already occurred in the conditioning framework of industrialization. By the end of the nine-teenth century the primitive accumulation required to start up an adequate process of industrialization had changed. Market opportunities had changed, as had the very structure of markets. The dimensions of the effort required to enter the industrial area had become much larger and the difficulties far greater. With the crisis of 1873 the spectre of excess productive capacity appeared within capitalist economies. The increase in the supply of agricultural produce created critical conditions for European agriculture; the resulting significant diminution of agricul-tural incomes caused a contraction in effective demand and hence a restriction of markets. Competition became more acute. Economies of scale were sought for in order to achieve a reduction of costs and hence greater competitive power by technical and productive concentration. Attempts to seize markets became necessary, and economic initiative looked for political support. The interdependence of the sectors of the economy increased enormously, and growth based primarily on one sector – the textile industry, or railways – was replaced by multi-sectoral advance. New methods needed to be introduced to raise capital. Heavy technical concentration, a higher capital intensity per worker, required greater funds. While the small enterprises of the early period of indus-trialization could often meet their needs by self-financing, the new highly concentrated enterprises had to turn to the capital market. Joint-

[1] E. L. Jones, 'Introduction' to *Agriculture and Economic Growth in England, 1650–1815* (London, 1967) p. 1.

stock companies developed, the stock-market and the mixed deposit-investment bank grew in importance. The state began to adopt protectionist policies.[1]

It is clear that this is a wholly different world from that in which England found herself at the moment of her industrial revolution. This essay is not directly concerned with the economic, or indeed the political consequences of the creation of an industrial base in Italy under these conditions. What I wish to emphasize is the role entrusted to agriculture, a role sanctioned by the customs tariff of 1888 which introduced a high duty on imported wheat and flour. The free-trade economists in Italy denounced the negative effect that this defence of domestic cereal production would have on the cost of living. The effect was, in fact, that the home market (already suffering from the impact of American grain exports) contracted still further at the very moment when the pace of industrialization was to be forced – not only in heavy industry (iron and steel) but also in a consumer goods industry (cotton). The protective cereal tariff also meant a definite renunciation of agricultural progress based on the development of livestock systems in the agricultural sector. The backward areas, from the point of view of agriculture, were to remain backward. The high degree of territorial concentration of industrial production further limited the expansion of the home market, introducing an element of permanent rigidity in effective demand. Because its possibilities of progress had been blocked, Italian agriculture was to remain a deadweight on economic expansion. The crisis which checked Italian economic development in the early 1960s must be attributed in good part, in my opinion, to the bottlenecks and inflationary tendencies provoked by the agricultural sector, which led to the serious deficit in the balance of payments. In practice, Italian agriculture in the last eighty years – that is, during the first and second industrial 'take-off' – does not appear to have made sufficient strides forward to enable one to think of it as a progressing sector, not even progressing (as would be normal) at a slower rhythm than the industrial sector.

Does this mean, in theoretical terms, that agriculture can be considered as a 'substitutive' factor of economic development? I doubt it. Historical observation suggests that a general, continuous, maintained process of economic development has never occurred without an expanding agricultural sector. Examples of discontinuous, jerky development,

[1] On this point, see the acute remarks of L. Cafagna, 'L'industrializzazione italiana. La formazione di una "base industriale" fra il 1896 e il 1914', in *Studi storici*, a. II (1961) n. 3–4, pp. 690 ff.

with serious territorial and social disequilibria, can be found. But these very examples underline the necessity of agricultural development. Errors of perspective derive from a failure to take account of historical details. A model of the English type (increase of agricultural productivity and production – transfer of resources from the agricultural to the industrial sector – industrial 'take-off' – in a logical, but not necessarily temporal sequence) can be useful to understand how the process occurred in different ways in various countries, what the differences are, what different results have been achieved. But superimposing such a model on the empirical data deforms the historical reality in Italy, France, Germany. It is equally erroneous to disaggregate the model and substitute its parts. Given certain premises, certain conditions follow. But different premises are followed by different consequences, by another type of industrialization, an industrial complex endowed with its own peculiarities, particular types of relationships between industry and banks, between economic and public power, a specific territorial pattern, a specific employment structure.

The first error I have mentioned was one into which Professor R. Romeo fell when discussing Italian industrialization.[1] On the basis of an incorrect reading of historical statistics, he asserted that an increase of agricultural production and incomes formed the source of primitive accumulation in the first two decades after Unity (1860–80); that is, the source of capital which financed the necessary infrastructure for subsequent industrialization. It has been shown that there was no significant improvement in agricultural production and incomes in these two decades. It seems clear to me that Romeo was 'obliged' to read the statistics wrongly by a *schema* or classical model that he had in mind, and which he wished to apply to the Italian case at all costs, considering the Italian case as a successful, although belated, example of industrialization. In fact, as I stated earlier, the delay in Italian industrialization changed all or almost all the aspects of the problem. Moreover, it was an unsuccessful form of industrialization, if I can express myself thus, a distorted, dualistic, partial process of industrialization, compared with that of the 'first-comers'.

There is also the mistake of disaggregating the model and substituting its parts. This is a more sophisticated mistake. Professor A. Gerschenkron has applied his theory of substitutive factors to Italian development, maintaining that the necessary supply of capital to start an industrial spurt could not have come simply from private wealth formed in the

[1] R. Romeo, *Risorgimento e capitalismo* (Bari, 1959) pp. 111 ff.

primary sector, but from the banks and state finance.[1] Variations and alternatives depend on the different degrees of backwardness of the individual countries. I think it is correct to underline that a strategic role can be exercised by different forms of mobilizing capital. But in all probability the supply of capital – in contrast to Gerschenkron's view – is not the sole condition of an industrial revolution.

It is true that the intensification of productive capital is the obligatory route for any substantial spurt in *per capita* output, but a model of growth cannot limit itself to highlighting a single causal element, it cannot be reduced to a simple capital accumulation model, or else it risks ending up as a tautology. One cannot ignore the problem of the supply of labour, whether it came from previous employment in agriculture, 'expelled' from agriculture to use the Marxist expression, or from a net increase of population. In both cases agriculture's task will be to provide an increase of food supplies. Nor can one ignore the problem of supplies of raw materials – which means that agriculture is again a crucial factor. But, as is well known, other variables can be identified in a process of growth: formation of 'human capital', market opportunities, political conditions, legislation. None of these variables can be taken in a unilateral manner; each must be considered as an integral part of a complex unitary process. The major or minor weight exerted by one or another variable in a given historical case of growth does not mean that the variables can be reciprocally substituted, as if they would produce substantially homogeneous results; it means that there are different types of growth, according to the historical conditions, the period and the place. But in no instance can the absence of important factors – such as an available supply of qualified labour or the support of agriculture – be compensated by the presence of others. The consequences of such an absence have always been extremely negative, delaying growth, or preventing it from achieving all its principal objectives.

I hope it is clear that what I have said does not refer to the controversy over the existence, or non-existence, of a leading sector in the process of growth. Even following the leading sector theory, one cannot deny the supporting and transference function exercised by the entire economy. But when the support and transferences are weak, the entire process develops hesitant and distorted characteristics. Of course the prerequisites and conditions of growth are not uniform. I wholeheartedly agree with this point, which has been considerably clarified by American

---

[1] A. Gerschenkron, *Economic Backwardness in Historical Perspective* (Cambridge, Mass., 1962) pp. 87–8.

27

scholars in the last few years. But what these scholars have often neglected is that neither are the results uniform. While one can agree with Dr Hartwell that the English industrial revolution was a case of balanced growth,[1] it is difficult to believe that balanced growth occurred in Italy or Japan. What seems to me important is that essential elements in the preparation and then in the course of growth cannot be substituted. They can be absent or barely present, but this will inevitably provoke serious consequences in the entire process. It did in Italy.

Even if one were to agree with Professor Gerschenkron that a decisive role was played in Italian growth at the end of the nineteenth century by the supply of capital, it would still be necessary to explain where the wealth mobilized by the banks had been formed previously. For banks do not create wealth; they merely collect and distribute it. It seems to me that Professor Gerschenkron has neglected the function of state finances: they constituted a powerful mobilizer of capital in Italy, transferring it from agriculture to the infrastructure, both through taxation and through the public debt. But agriculture, which was flourishing in no region and was in a very poor condition in some regions, suffered heavily from this haemorrhage. In part, the capital consisted of the accumulated wealth of landed proprietors; in part it consisted of resources extracted from peasants and leaseholders, and so withdrawn from consumption and investment. One has to admit that Italian historiography has tended to study this problem mostly from the social viewpoint, examining the condition of misery of the rural populations after unification in order to explain the causes of the insurrections which broke out sporadically in the countryside. But it is easy to understand the economic result of this primitive fiscal policy: contraction of internal demand, a serious obstacle to the formation of a national market.

Recent discussion has clarified the importance of the existence of a national market and its capacity to respond to the impulses of industrialization. Italy in the second half of the nineteenth century had barely achieved political unity, it was struggling to unify the administration, the legal system, transportation. The standard of living, which was already low, fell further almost everywhere in the countryside, because of the fiscal measures as well as the agrarian crisis. The cereal tariff protected incomes from foreign price competition, but did not improve the position of peasant families, who lived mainly in conditions of

---

[1] R. M. Hartwell, 'Introduction' to *The Causes of the Industrial Revolution in England* (London, 1967) p. 15.

28

subsistence, with little contact with the market, in north-east, central and southern Italy. Nor was agriculture expanding in the more advanced regions, as we shall see, although it had reached positions of considerable modernity in some sectors some time before. My opinion, which I can only outline here, is that agricultural backwardness is the key to understanding many of the distinctive characteristics of Italian economic development in its first phase – between the end of the nineteenth and the early twentieth centuries – and also later.

Italian agriculture, all considered, was unable to supply the necessary resources to create the conditions for an industrial take-off. What it gave, in financial terms, was torn from it more or less coercively; one should remember that entire regions lived in a virtual state of siege for some decades after Unity. In consequence, as already stated, agricultural demand for industrial products was restricted, creating an obstacle to a balanced and continuous industrial expansion which was not overcome for half a century.

At this point it is necessary to examine the conditions of Italian agriculture more directly. There is no doubt that its regional and local characteristics differ considerably: hence it is impossible to trace a unitary history. Let us limit ourselves to the more advanced regions, which are also better documented. What strikes one most is the precocity of certain developments. It has been stated that high farming was an integral part of industrialization in England,[1] which meant (if I understand correctly) that the agronomic revolution, or at least its high point, and the industrial revolution in England were aspects of a single, common process of growth. In Lombardy an agronomic revolution occurred some centuries before the industrial take-off. It is true that problems of chronology have been raised about English agriculture as well in the last fifteen years: the turning-point, which was traditionally dated after the middle of the eighteenth century, has been taken back by some scholars.[2] But all in all, compared to other countries, I think one can assert that the processes were reasonably contemporaneous. They were preceded by what one might call a structural and social preparation – by what has been called 'the secularization of the soil' in the sixteenth and early seventeenth centuries – 'when the medieval past, as represented by the hold on the land of the Church, was abruptly discarded'. Then, and immediately after, occurred the first evident progress of agrarian

[1] Hartwell, loc. cit., p. 17.
[2] E. L. Jones, *Agriculture and Economic Growth*, cit.; E. Kerridge, *The Agricultural Revolution* (London, 1967).

29

technology.[1] It is widely admitted that this development acquired a breadth which was no longer local towards the mid-eighteenth century. From then on a modern agriculture and a modern industry progressed together. To a foreigner, this is a fairly unified process, even if English historians, who are examining it more closely, tend to underline the intermediate phases and the irregularities.

By comparison, the developments of Italian agriculture were far more irregular and prolonged. They were marked by far longer pauses, and even regressions, which followed periods of undeniably rapid progress. A flow of resources from the agricultural to the industrial sector, necessary to achieve industrial 'take-off', was never of significance, or at least never occurred at the right time and on the necessary scale. One should note that the Po valley never experienced the great secular crisis which hit the countryside throughout Europe from the first decades of the fourteenth century. Nevertheless the results of the great increases in productivity which occurred in the agriculture of the Po valley between the fourteenth and the sixteenth centuries, which in some ways lay at the base of the great expansion of urban life and of Italian society and culture, were not transmitted to industry, did not give industry a jolt, a progressive push, and in the final analysis were dispersed during the crisis of the seventeenth century.

It is necessary to point out the key dates of Italian agricultural history from the year 1000 in order to clarify the precocity of certain developments as well as the long periods of stagnation and the type of obstacles encountered in stimulating a general process of expansion. For example, the phenomenon of a 'transfusion of trading capital' in agriculture 'allied . . . to new farming practices', which occurred from the mid-seventeenth century in England, as Dr E. L. Jones has noted,[2] was already well known in northern and central Italy in the fourteenth century. Italian scholars today reject the idea that the search for land by commercial capital which occurred in the fourteenth and fifteenth centuries was simply a retreat from trading activities, a total loss to economic growth, as the older economic historians believed. The switch of capital to land used to be seen as one of the main causes of the Italian decadence of the following centuries. But in reality the investment of new capital started off a wave of technical and productive advances, and gave birth to a tough 'agrarian capitalism'. Earlier, at least from the

[1] J. Thirsk, 'Farming Techniques', in *The Agrarian History of England and Wales*, IV (1500–1640) (Cambridge, 1967).
[2] E. L. Jones, *Agriculture and Economic Growth*, cit., p. 6.

thirteenth century, ecclesiastical estates were beginning to break up. Thus commercial capital found no serious institutional obstacles in its path and managed to take possession of the land in decisive regions, such as Tuscany and Lombardy.[1]

Italian medievalists of the old school have been fascinated by urban history. As a result, research on Italian medieval agriculture has suffered badly, but from what we already know we can argue that the first signs of an agricultural revival were extraordinarily early. Between the ninth and the tenth centuries, as is well known, metals were hardly used in Europe in agricultural tools. Ploughing equipment was normally constructed by the peasants at home, and Professor Duby believes that they made poor wooden instruments. But in Lombardy the *ferrarii* appear extremely often in noble inventories, and many villages were held to make regular payments in iron. Similarly, the substitution of money payments by labour services and payments in kind is to be found in the later ninth and in the tenth centuries more frequently in northern Italy than elsewhere. In the same period in many Bavarian fiefs money payments were unknown. What was happening was the transformation of the noble fief itself in this part of Italy. The peasants who cultivated the soil received it on perpetual quit-rent (*a livello*). There were few *corvées*. The traditional direct domanial exploitation of the soil was already giving way to share-cropping and leaseholding. By the eleventh century great enterprises were extending the cultivable area. The large communes took part in works of drainage, irrigation, land improvements, often contributing decisively to the 'agrarian conquest'. The increase of agricultural production, which the documents show almost everywhere in western Europe between the twelfth and fourteenth centuries, seems to be due more to the extension of the area of arable land than to substantial improvements in rotations, but it is probable that in northern-central Italy there were also increases in productivity. The preparation of the soil certainly improved, while traction became more powerful through new methods of harnessing the oxen. As a result of technological innovations, the importance of the plough grew in agricultural work, land fell in price in comparison to the cost of animals. The existence of important cities influenced the neighbouring countryside in varying ways. The sale of agricultural produce was concentrated within the cities, thus causing a decline in the village markets. Peasant obligations to provide artisan services in rural domestic industries vanished early

---

[1] C. M. Cipolla, 'Introduzione' to *Storia dell'economia italiana*, I (Torino, 1959) pp. 15 ff.

because of the emergence in the cities of small-scale mercantile production, which offered better quality goods at cheaper prices. The
communes took over the rights of the *signoria* (prerogatives which were
based on possession of the soil), while in other regions of western Europe
such rights remained in feudal hands. It is probable that this original
interdependence of relations between city and countryside accounts for
the capacity of the Po valley to resist the long crisis of the fourteenth
century, and so prolong its exceptional demographic and economic
expansion until the end of the fifteenth century. But feudalism, stripped
of its basis of personal relationships, and with the feudal lords obliged
to abandon their direct exploitation of the soil, survived in intermediary
social relations, in the very organization of urban life, in the incapacity
of the cities to overcome fragmentation into small local units. The new
lords who inherited communal power could not find the strength to
become national monarchs.

Thus, we may ask, is it within agriculture, or outside it, that one must
search for the obstacles which prevented the use of agricultural progress
from stimulating general development? What prevented the accumulated
resources of the lower Lombard plain from producing all-round expansion? Did a demographic explosion occur? Were incomes eaten up by a
mechanism of conspicuous consumption; and, if so, what mechanism?
Why were other more profitable and productive possibilities of investment lacking? It is still too early to find a reply to these questions in
contemporary Italian historiography, but there can be no doubt that
there was an exceptionally early and deeply progressive advance in
agriculture. It is difficult to believe that Lombard agriculture, in the
fourteenth and fifteenth centuries, could not already have ensured the
necessary supplies of food and raw materials for an industrial 'take-off'
in the region. But perhaps this was its limit: it would inevitably have
been an expansion on a regional base, on too restricted a base, insufficient
to offer all the necessary responses to a process of industrialization,
however favoured by circumstances. So one returns to the theme of a
national market. Four centuries were to pass before the political premises
for the creation of a national market were to be laid. And the political
premises were then far from fulfilling the entire range of necessary
conditions. This point allows one to note, in passing, the weakness of
the thesis current today that the north of Italy owed nothing to the south
for its industrial development this century. Why in that case, one may
ask, did the northern regions not begin that growth, since it may be
assumed that they already possessed the internal requirements? Why

did this growth only occur after Unity, after the effects of Unity were felt?

But let us return for a moment to consider the degree of progress achieved by Lombard agriculture in the Middle Ages. The problem has attracted the attention of a number of scholars in recent years and they have managed to shed some light on it. It is enough to remember that only eight years ago Slicher van Bath completely neglected Italy in his *Agrarian History of Western Europe*, except on one particular point, to note how much our knowledge of this subject has advanced. Dr P. J. Jones has made various important contributions to the argument.[1] He has underlined the fact that medieval agriculture, even during the periods of its major development, was based more on the exploitation of labour than on the use of capital and advanced techniques. From this point of view the Italian case fits in well with the overall tendencies of European agriculture. But if there was no agronomic revolution, there was, he writes, 'a certain radical progress of Italian agriculture', a movement which not only extended the cultivated area, but intensified the methods of agriculture. This movement began in the tenth century and lasted for some centuries. Thus the medieval agronomists 'did not limit themselves to copying the Roman authorities; and the techniques that they describe, or that are revealed by other sources, not only re-established, but in certain points surpassed the best of Roman practices'.[2] Among the innovations one should note the introduction of new crops. The introduction of rice is particularly important, because it came at the same time as the successful employment of new techniques of irrigation. These are also the centuries of the expansion of the vine, which was 'accompanied by technical advances and, still more, by a diversity of production',[3] because, after the disappearance of the old varieties, new ones were created by selection or importation. There were advances in rotational methods, and here we touch upon a type of innovation affecting the whole system of agriculture, and hence possessing a revolutionary potential. Fallow land, in fact, was suppressed in certain areas of the northern regions and replaced, probably from the fourteenth century, by systems of continuous cultivation, or sown with fodder crops, especially vegetable crops. To this one can add the improvement of ploughs

[1] P. J. Jones, 'Per la storia agraria italiana nel Medio Evo: lineamenti e problemi', in *Rivista storica italiana* (1964); 'Medieval Agrarian Society in its prime. Italy', in *The Cambridge Economic History of Europe*, I: *The Agrarian Life of the Middle Ages* (Cambridge, 1966) 2nd ed.

[2] P. J. Jones, 'Per la storia agraria italiana', cit., p. 313.

[3] Ibid., p. 314.

33

and the development of new methods of processing agricultural products.

Although the theme has still not been sufficiently studied, I should like to suggest that the transformation introduced in methods of rotation constituted a fundamental change in medieval agricultural practices and a remarkable anticipation of a process which only began in the Low Countries in the mid-fifteenth century. It is true that a form of convertible husbandry is documented for the Ghent zone as early as 1326, and it was certainly practised in Flanders around 1368. But it consisted in tilling the land for a time and then using it as pasture for a number of years. The succession also included one year fallow; only in the seventeenth century was the grassland replaced by clover. The cultivation of fodder crops is only documented from about 1480.[1] A system of continuous rotation on irrigated land was, in contrast, probably the main technical support of Lombard agriculture during the years of the long crisis of the fourteenth and fifteenth centuries. One can presume that the general tendency of prices in these two centuries of European history favoured a process of modernization, that the availability of capital and the presence of active entrepreneurial forces acted with a vigour unknown in other countries. It is well known that from the early decades of the fourteenth century a heavy fall in cereal prices occurred; butter, meat and fat prices stood their ground more firmly. The high price of wool had radical consequences. Arable land went back to grass in many places. In parts of England many farmers changed over from arable to stock farming, and especially to sheep farming. Spanish sheep farming was at its height in the late Middle Ages; the Merinos provided great quantities of wool for export. In Germany, as in England, corn fields were turned over to sheep farming. The period saw the great spread of dairy farms in the Tyrol and Styria. Given this general pattern one can understand how systems of agriculture based on meadows and where possible on fodder crops asserted themselves. As Slicher van Bath writes, 'it is worthy of note, however, that these new systems were nearly all first heard of in the fourteenth and fifteenth centuries, a period particularly favourable to animal husbandry'.[2]

In Italy, however, wool production was never a motive force of agricultural development, except round Pisa where it occurred in the second half of the thirteenth century. Here, it is worth noting, the consequences

[1] B. H. Slicher van Bath, *The Agrarian History of Western Europe. A.D. 500–1850* (London, 1963) p. 179.
[2] Ibid.

were as in England: emigration of the rural population and deserted villages. In the north, and especially in Lombardy, the motive force was the production of dairy produce. Already in the nineteenth century Carlo Cattaneo asserted that in Lombardy certain principles of high farming had been applied in the late Middle Ages before they passed from Flanders to England.[1] Many foreign observers in the eighteenth and nineteenth centuries acknowledged the great modernity of Lombard agriculture: Arthur Young, Symonds, Burger. The reason for this, as Professor Romani has suggested, was that certain systems, such as the use of water-meadows in the Milanese and the inclusion of fodder crops in the rotation, were so ancient that they did not seem worth while boasting about to the Lombards of those centuries.[2] In fact, the first Italian to outline the progress of Lombard agriculture was Cattaneo, who claimed that the Lombard lands, which once had been covered by marshes and broken up by mountains and lakes, had become the best in Europe through the work of many centuries. The researches of Professor Cipolla and Professor Romani have shown that this work began very early and was favoured by, and in its turn sustained, the uninterrupted expansion of agricultural production in Lombardy, even during the years of the great fourteenth to fifteenth century depression. An indirect confirmation of this thesis, which still requires further research, is offered by a study of the deserted villages in Italy carried out by Christiane Klapisch-Zuber and John Day.[3] Villages were abandoned in Sicily, Sardinia, the countryside around Rome and the Tuscan Maremma from the thirteenth and fourteenth centuries, although the crisis perhaps only reached its peak later. In contrast there was apparently no similar crisis, but a stable situation in northern Italy and in notable parts of Tuscany, such as the countryside around Florence. This continued agricultural prosperity would help to explain the 'long period' of wealth enjoyed by the Italian cities. For they could not have survived so prosperously until the sixteenth century solely on the incomes of their undoubtedly remunerative international trade, nor was industry so developed that it could have replaced agriculture as the supplier of a surplus on which urban centres such as Siena and Florence, Bologna and Milan, lived and prospered.

What still remains to be explained in large part is why so developed an agriculture did not succeed in providing the impulse for an early

[1] Cited by M. Romani, *L'Agricoltura in Lombardia dal periodo delle riforme al 1859* (Milano, 1957) p. 23.

[2] Ibid., pp. 16–17.

[3] C. Klapisch-Zuber – J. Day, 'Villages désertés en Italie', in *Villages désertés et histoire économique. XI–XVIII siècles* (Paris, 1965) pp. 419–59.

industrial revolution. Certain of the essential prerequisites, supplied specifically by agriculture, existed: there was no shortage of qualified labour – it is enough to think of the Tuscan textile industry or the Lombard armament and iron industries, or the Venetian shipbuilding industry. Where were the obstacles to a general economic development? As I have said, they were probably in the absence of a national state, in the impossibility of creating an adequate home market, in the presence of seriously backward regions. These causes can be judged as exercising a decisive negative weight on the possibilities of an industrialization *avant la lettre* in Italy. For I do not believe that technological backwardness or lack of energy could be regarded as insuperable barriers. The English industrial revolution, it has been noted, 'hardly depended at all on scientific and technological advances which were not already available in the sixteenth century'.[1] We know of the great wealth of inventions of Italian Renaissance scientists which remained on paper. It is, and will probably remain, impossible to quantify the amounts of energy and innovation necessary for an industrial expansion at given moments, even with the advantage of historical hindsight.

At all events, in the seventeenth century the country plunged into economic decline, which in some regions was accompanied by a deep process of refeudalization. Even in Lombardy part of the medieval advance was probably lost. But capital investment, particularly in the intensive network of irrigation canals, the 'building up of the soil' by the productive forces of capitalism, created a patrimony which in Lombardy, after crises and disasters, was to yield fruit in future centuries. In the eighteenth century, when a new period of progress began, the predominant feature of the Lombard countryside was large productive units run by wage labour, while the crop system was integrated with the raising of livestock in a considerable part of the plain, and an industry based on dairy farming. In the Milanese water-meadows were extremely widespread. About 1760, lands under rotation covered more than a fifth of the total cultivated area – 82 per cent in the plains around Pavia, Cremona and Lodi, where they were concentrated. In certain of the provinces of Piedmont there were similar successes. Almost a century later the area covered by fodder crops had increased in Lombardy by 80 per cent, the irrigated area had been further enlarged, covering 40, 60 and 72 per cent of the plains around Cremona, Pavia and Lodi respectively. The cultivation of mulberries had been

---

[1] E. J. Hobsbawm, 'Il secolo XVII nello sviluppo del capitalismo', in *Studi storici*, I (1959–60) n. 4, p. 665.

intensified in the hilly areas, but had also been extended to the plain, particularly between the Adda river and the Veneto. Output of rice and maize increased, rye declined, wheat remained stationary.[1] Most successful of all was what Verri had defined as the *cultura a caci*, based on fodder and cows.

The movement of prices between the eighteenth and nineteenth centuries is significant. Against the basic weakness of wheat prices can be seen a continuous expansion of demand and price rise for rice, silk and cheeses. This directed agricultural activities towards the market 'with the certainty of positive results which in the long term was even pernicious', as Professor Romani has written, because this certainly distracted producers from all thought of technical improvements. This lies at the heart of that lack of technical interest by the propertied classes, that attitude of incomprehension about the drive towards the 'new agriculture' that came from France, and above all from England: for it was not and did not seem new, at least in the irrigated Lombard plain, because, as we have seen, the abolition of fallow periods and the rotation of fodder and grain had already begun to be employed in the Middle Ages. The result of being *avant-garde* was a deafness towards the methods which returned from abroad, enriched and improved. The enrichment and improvement consisted in the fact that continuous cultivation and good rotation had shown themselves possible and beneficial in England on dry lands, whereas the Lombard proprietors continued to maintain that it was a system restricted to irrigated soils. In the dry plain in Italy agronomic progress did not affect pasture-land, but limited itself above all to mulberry and silk-worm production. In this part of the region, as in the rest of the country, the secular deficiencies of inadequate fertilizers, weak oxen and low yields survived. The 'great truth that high farming is independent of irrigation', which according to Cattaneo[2] was the discovery of the English, took a long time to penetrate Lombardy and the rest of Italy. As can be seen from this brief description, while a large part of Italian agriculture in the eighteenth and early nineteenth centuries remained backward, the more advanced areas existed almost like oases without connection with the rest of the country, without an ability to exercise any real influence on the country's productive tendencies, and tied for the most part to an external market which accentuated their pre-existing characteristics.

[1] Romani, *L'Agricoltura in Lombardia*, cit., p. 27.
[2] C. Cattaneo, 'Dell'agricoltura inglese paragonata alla nostra', in *Saggi di economia rurale* (Torino, 1939) p. 308.

D

It is certainly not chance that when the first industrial spurt took place at the end of the nineteenth century, it occurred in regions like Lombardy and Piedmont where a previous process of agricultural development had to some degree occurred. But one needs to note the delay in this spurt and the incapacity of Italian industrialization to acquire a national spread. If there is anything 'national' in Italian industrialization, in fact, it is its particular propensity to utilize resources (both financial and human) from every region in order to accelerate progress in limited areas, concentrating both the effort and the results there. In the early 1960s, when Italian industry began a second and more powerful advance, this characteristic remained the same.

Rather than conclusions or definitive statements, I have preferred in this essay to point to problems, elements of fact, initial comments, which reflect the state of research, which in many respects is still in its infancy. What seems reasonably clear to me is the existence of a singular relationship between agriculture and economic development in Italy. This was a basically negative relationship, in the sense that agriculture, all considered, has never managed to sustain a regular and general growth: it has provided a land to be sacked rather than a source of resources to be purchased, the proceeds from which could have expanded the rural market for industrial goods. The Mezzogiorno and some regions of central and northern Italy did not share in the growth when it occurred, nor did they draw benefit from it; indeed they suffered from it by the obligatory withdrawal of wealth and labour and were left in a worse state. From A. Lewis to W. W. Rostow, British and American scholars have considered an increase in the rate of investment as decisive for an industrial 'take-off'. This lies at the basis of a fashionable current opinion in Italy that any means of lifting wealth out of agriculture, even if by simple robbery, is an adequate way of starting up and sustaining growth. The misleading if not abusive name of 'primitive accumulation' has sometimes been applied to this withdrawal of wealth. But, in fact, this robbery kills the goose that lays the golden eggs, and checks or limits the formation of an agricultural market for industry.

As Maddison has pointed out, the relationship between investment and increased production is not uniform; wide differences can be noted between the experiences of different nations and even of the same nation in different periods. An industry in its early stages, as Bairoch has written, probably requires inconsiderable investment. In the eighteenth century a major source of capital for industry was apparently reinvested profits: 'in other words the rate of investment was dependent on the rate of growth'.[1] Perhaps Hartwell exaggerates slightly. Empirical evidence shows that things are not that easy, that the financing of growth met with checks and deviations, that the impeccable mechanism of such formulae often exists only in the minds of economists. Thus, while Hartwell underlines reinvested profits, Pressnell has pointed (perhaps with equal exaggeration) to the part played by country banking in financing the English industrial revolution.[2] The problem would appear to be more related to the mobilization of savings, to the propensities of savers, than to the quantity of investable funds. From the quantitative point of view, I imagine that Professor Postan is right when he states that 'at the beginning of the eighteenth century there were enough wealthy people in the country to finance an economic effort far greater than the modest activities of the makers of the industrial revolution'.[3] One could probably show that a similar situation existed in Italy in the fifteenth century. Today, a wholly different rate of capital formation is required, but this is not the important point. What matters is not a large volume of monetary wealth, which after all exists in some backward countries (e.g. oil-producing countries) without having the least effect on their economic growth, but the social process of separating the workers from the means of production, the concentration of the latter in the hands of a class of capitalist entrepreneurs, the creation of a market. This lies at the basis of all mechanisms of capitalist economic growth.

The role of agriculture in this is clear: it makes a labour force available, thanks to the breakdown of feudal ties and the increase of productivity, and it increases the demand for both consumption and investment goods by the increase of income and the creation of new needs within the family and the farm. A positive role of this kind was not exercised by Italian agriculture. The one exception was the rich agriculture of the Po valley. Here agriculture early produced a surplus, but did not find the generally favourable conditions in which to employ its surplus. This might have formed the condition for an industrial advance; instead churches and palaces absorbed the greater part. Here was an agriculture which, resting on the laurels of its previous progress, proved incapable in the eighteenth and nineteenth centuries of developing much further, and so stayed, surrounded by a backward Italy.

[1] Hartwell, 'The Causes of the Industrial Revolution: an Essay in Methodology', in *The Causes of the Industrial Revolution in England*, cit., p. 67.

[2] L. S. Pressnell, *Country Banking in the Industrial Revolution* (Oxford, 1954).

[3] M. Postan, 'Recent Trends in the Accumulation of Capital', in the *Econ. Hist. Rev.*, VI (1935) n. 1, p. 2.

2 Landownership and economic growth in England in the eighteenth century

F. M. L. THOMPSON

The idea that economic growth in England was an integrated process, rather than a somewhat fortuitous collection of changes in individual segments of the economy, has made a striking impression on the activities of economic historians in recent years. Very naturally those who have taken up this task of analysing and displaying the inter-connectedness of the various limbs of the economy have concentrated in the first place on the major variables – those most in favour are capital accumulation or investment, innovation (whether agricultural or industrial), export markets, internal demand and population; or they have looked at the major sectors of the economy, such as agriculture.[1] In this state of affairs it is not surprising that such an apparently specialized and narrow topic as the relationship of landownership to economic growth has yet to acquire a formal literature, even though there have been several important contributions to the elucidation of particular problems that involve connections between the behaviour of landowners and the course and level of sections of economic activity.[2]

Nevertheless, given the central position occupied by land in the pre-industrial economy, and the crucial role which property in a rather wider sense has played and continues to play in industrializing and advanced economies, sooner or later an attempt will have to be made to appraise the general role of the landed system in the development of the economy as a whole. Such an appraisal ought to be divided into three

---

[1] See in particular M. W. Flinn, *Origins of the Industrial Revolution* (1966); R. M. Hartwell, *The Causes of the Industrial Revolution in England* (1967); and E. L. Jones, *Agriculture and Economic Growth in England, 1650–1815* (1967).

[2] Apart from those contributions specifically discussed below, the following works should be mentioned: J. D. Chambers, 'Enclosure and Labour Supply in the Industrial Revolution', *Econ. Hist. Rev.*, 2nd ser., V (1953); H. J. Habakkuk, 'Economic Functions of Landowners in the Seventeenth and Eighteenth Centuries', *Explorations in Entrepreneurial History*, VI (1952); G. E. Mingay, 'The Size of Farms in the Eighteenth Century', *Econ. Hist. Rev.*, 2nd ser., XIV (1962).

parts. It should consider in turn the structure of landownership and estate distribution and their economic linkages; the role of the landowners and their immediate dependants, both as producers and consumers; and the wider derived and indirect effects of the system. The aim of this paper, after a fashion which it is perhaps becoming a trifle pernicious to follow, is to state this general agenda, and then to confine itself to the more modest and preliminary task of scrutinizing some of the propositions which have been advanced on these matters. It may be that by weighing them against such quantitative evidence as is available, examining the implications of the arguments and assumptions on which they rest, and suggesting some areas for further investigation, the issues will be made less obscure and the direction of future research will be made clearer.

This is not the occasion on which to challenge my own conclusion about the course of changes in the distribution of land by estate-size groups since the sixteenth century.[1] Broadly that conclusion was that in the four centuries following 1500 the distribution between the great landowners (with estates of around 10,000 acres and upwards), the gentry and squirearchy (with between 300 and 10,000 acres apiece), and the small landowners (with less than 300 acres each) remained remarkably stable, altered only slowly, and does not appear to have been subject to any sudden and dramatic shifts. As far as general conclusions emerge from J. P. Cooper's latest contribution, it would appear to confirm and extend backward from 1500 one element in the structure, by making the share of the great landowners pretty well constant since 1436. It would also seem to make the share of the small owners a larger one in 1500, and possibly a growing one in the sixteenth and seventeenth centuries, thus at one stroke severely deflating both the 'rise of the gentry' and the sixteenth-century agonies of the peasantry. It might also be thought to have played a conjuring trick on the monastic and crown lands, which seem to have disappeared without leaving a trace. But although it rightly encourages all of us to treat Gregory King's estimates for the late seventeenth century with a great deal more scepticism than they have generally received, since they now appear in many particulars to have been numbers thought up to fit in with – or not quite fit in with – sums previously, and in successive versions differently, concocted, Cooper's article still does not leave us with any pronounced shifts in the overall

[1] F. M. L. Thompson, 'The Social Distribution of Landed Property in England since the Sixteenth Century', *Econ. Hist. Rev.*, 2nd ser., XIX (1966) pp. 505–17.

structure in the seventeenth century which could then be construed as imparting momentum to the economy.[1]

My structure does allow for some decline in the small owners' share after 1690, and it is possibly at this point that the 'general stability' thesis is most vulnerable. If such a decline, at such a point of time, was fairly sharp and fairly swift, then it might indeed bear some causal relationship to the Jones-Kerridge agricultural revolution of fodder crops and live-stock which was in progress in the 1650–1750 period.[2] For a switch out of peasant-subsistence holdings – regardless of the destination of these holdings in ownership terms – would mean an increase in the proportion of commercially tenanted holdings. A greater number of tenant farmers, or simply a greater area of tenanted land, would mean that an increased proportion of total agricultural output moved into the orbit of the market. The incentives of all commercial farmers, not merely those of any additions to their numbers produced by such a process of peasant decline, would thus be magnified; incentives to meet their rents and increase or maintain their incomes in the face of falling prices, or of shifts in relative crop prices, incentives whose bidding would lead to an acceleration and extension of those features of the agricultural revolution which have been observed.

Habakkuk has argued for just such a decline of the peasantry, between 1660 and 1740.[3] The argument is twofold. On the one hand, conditions became rough for peasant survival. The long sixteenth-century price rise halted, and agricultural prices fell, and then fluctuated violently between 1680 and 1720; and heavy land taxation, especially war taxation, fell on peasants as well as other landowners, and augmented the pressure to sell their holdings. In addition, growing attractions of alternative trading and commercial occupations tempted many small peasants, while they retained ownership of their holdings, to desert farming and leave it to tenants. On the other hand, conditions of relative shortage of land in the market, compared with the easy days of monastic, crown, church, and ruined-magnate lands in the abundantly supplied market of the sixteenth and early seventeenth centuries, forced those who

---

[1] J. P. Cooper, 'The Social Distribution of Land and Men in England, 1436–1700', *Econ. Hist. Rev.*, 2nd ser., XX (1967) pp. 419–40.

[2] E. L. Jones, *Agriculture and Economic Growth in England, 1650–1815* (1967); E. Kerridge, *The Agricultural Revolution* (1967). Kerridge, of course, argues that the technical changes were in progress for some considerable time before 1650.

[3] H. J. Habakkuk, 'La disparition du paysan anglais', *Annales*, XX (1965) pp. 649–63.

wanted to buy land to nibble at peasant holdings which they had earlier disdained so long as larger and tastier properties were freely available.

We must return to the implications of the land market argument presently. At the moment the point is that, although the argument for the occurrence of such a process of swift peasant decline at this crucial period is forceful and persuasive, no attempt has been made to measure it, and hence it is difficult to judge its significance as a possible force initiating agricultural innovation or tending to emphasize and magnify the extent of innovations already under way. It is perhaps excessively foolhardy, under the watchful eye of J. P. Cooper, to persist in pretending that Gregory King may be taken seriously – but in the era of aggregates and econometrics it still remains a tempting form of sin. For the total of what he termed the 'smaller freeholders' whose holdings seem to have averaged about 50 acres, Gregory King thought of a variety of numbers in 1688 and 1696, ranging from a low of 140,000 to a high of 400,000; in the light of the total acreage of England and the total acreage attributable to this group, mere credibility must incline us towards choosing the smaller of these figures.[1] Even so, more than 7 million acres in the hands of small peasants in 1690 may seem to constitute a very large reservoir of land that might have been released to commercial farming and agricultural innovations, until we remember that even in 1885 farms of under 50 acres still occupied nearly 4 million acres in all, so that even had every last small peasant owner disappeared, it would not have followed that small farms would also have vanished.[2] In any case, it has never been suggested that the entire class of small peasants were wiped out. The estimates of Joseph Massie for 1759–60, which are if possible less trustworthy than Gregory King's, allege that there were then 180,000 small freeholders – or, if we take the poorest group which he distinguishes, the freeholders with annual family incomes of £25, there were 120,000 of them.[3] In either case, little change in the size of this group between 1690 and 1760 seems to be allowed for, and, by inference, little change in the total acreage it possessed. Leaping forward to 1873, the somewhat different group of 'small proprietors' identified by Bateman, with estates of between 1 and 100 acres (therefore about the same as the derived estates of Massie's middling as well as his smallest freeholders, but larger than Gregory King's smaller freeholders)

[1] Tables printed in Appendix I to J. P. Cooper, loc. cit., pp. 436–8.

[2] Agricultural statistics for 1885, now most conveniently available in *A Century of Agricultural Statistics; Great Britain, 1866–1966*, H.M.S.O. (1968) p. 20.

[3] P. Mathias, 'The Social Structure in the Eighteenth Century: a calculation by Joseph Massie', *Econ. Hist. Rev.*, 2nd ser., X (1957) p. 42.

44

had over 200,000 members who between them owned nearly 4 million acres.[1]

Certainly these smallest landowners of the late nineteenth century were, for the most part, not the same people, were not from the same families, and did not have the same social and economic position as the smallest peasant owners of 1690; many of them, for instance, were owners of completely non-agricultural properties, and many others were non-farmers – such as butchers and retailers – or small absentee land-lords. Equally certainly, some quite sizeable chunk of land had, in aggregate, moved out of the possession of men whose properties made them fall into this estate-size group, at some time between 1690 and 1873; perhaps, on the extremely slender basis of the figures presented, as much as 3–4 million acres in all. But as we know that some such movement occurred in the post-1815 situation, and that some such process was a very common precursor to enclosure at any stage before 1815, perhaps we could guess that not more than half the shift had occurred before 1760 and in time to contribute to the Jones-Kerridge agricultural revolution. At this order of magnitude, the movement of $1\frac{1}{2}$–2 million acres out of the ownership of the smallest peasants, and the additional or concurrent movement of some proportion, but only a proportion, of this from small peasant-holdings into forming part of larger farms, could have made a definite contribution to facilitating the spread of innovations, but not, I would suppose, a decisive or initiating contribution. Indeed, I would be inclined to conclude that a shift of this order could well be presented as a consequence of the innovations – that is, the peasant response to the price situation produced by those innovations – and not as lying on the causal side at all.

If we turn now to those who Gregory King dubbed 'the better sort' of freeholders, whose estates are said to have averaged around 100–160 acres, we may obtain a somewhat different result. He insisted fairly stubbornly that there were 40,000 in this group, so that they might have controlled from 4 to 6 million acres. Massie thought that there were 30,000 of this better sort of freeholders in 1760, and with their assigned annual incomes of £100 per family their holdings must have been very much of a King-size. A perhaps spurious plausibility is lent to this trend by the fact that in 1873 there appear to have been 24,000 'lesser yeomen' landowners, with average estates of 170 acres, owning among them just over 4 million acres. Hence, if we could believe that 10,000 of this species

---

[1] J. Bateman's 'County Tables of Landowners', in G. C. Brodrick, *English Land and English Landlords* (1881, reprint 1968) pp. 173–87.

disappeared between 1690 and 1760, spiriting away with them into the possession of other and wealthier classes of landowners something between 1 and 1½ million acres which were already, at the moment of transference, parcelled up into comparatively large holdings of sizes convenient for the instant adoption of new husbandry without preliminary and expensive physical adaptation, then we might also believe that this particular shift in the structure of landownership was of some real moment in helping to shape and helping to cause the agricultural changes of this period.

Having set up this argument, it is interesting and perhaps totally deflating to note that Patrick Colquhoun in framing his 'General View of Society' in England and Wales in 1803, took over Gregory King's figures for both the better sort and the lesser freeholders without any alteration, that is he stated that in 1803 there were still 40,000 of the former and 120,000 of the latter, which he held to have been Gregory King's estimates for 1688.[1] Colquhoun certainly did not adopt these figures without giving them any thought, for he went out of his way to remark that 'there are certainly more freeholders than these stated as such; since, in the present times, almost every person who is in any degree opulent is also of this class'. We know now, from a number of local studies, that there was some post-enclosure tendency for the numbers of small owners to rise; and we also know that this trend was swollen during the French Wars when 'the rage for farming' led many small businessmen, traders, professional men and others to go into landed property in a small way in the hope of gaining a share of rising farm profits and of making capital gains.[2] It is therefore logically possible to interpret Colquhoun's figures as a faithful reflection of the reflux in small proprietors following a sag in their numbers in the first half of the eighteenth century as registered by Massie. But the second of these trends, if he had appreciated its existence, Colquhoun can be held to have discounted and deliberately excluded from his estimates; and in any case, this trend is only said to have commenced after about 1799. And in view of what contemporary opinion almost universally held to have been the effects of enclosures in diminishing the numbers of small owners, it is excessively unlikely that Colquhoun alone, and without himself thinking the matter worthy of explicit mention, had

[1] Patrick Colquhoun, *Treatise on Indigence* (1806) pp. 23–4.
[2] A. H. John, 'Farming in Wartime, 1793–1815', in E. L. Jones and G. E. Mingay (eds.), *Land, Labour and Population in the Industrial Revolution* (1967) pp. 44–6.

46

anticipated the results of modern historical research by arriving at a conclusion that enclosures had stimulated a resurgence of small properties.

It is therefore overwhelmingly probable that Colquhoun repeated the Gregory King figures, not unthinkingly, but because he knew of no reason for supposing that the numbers of genuine small freeholders had altered significantly between 1688 and 1801. In which case, any alteration in their numbers and in their relative importance as a landowning group which took place between 1688 and 1873 presumably took place after 1801 – which in effect, since we know that until 1815 conditions continued to favour the growth of small properties, means after 1815. Though, on other grounds, we may cast doubt on the credibility of all Colquhoun's estimates of the sizes of the different groups of landowners – the gentry, his 'knights' and 'squires' with average rentals of £1,500, have 29 per cent of the total land; and the great landowners, his 'peers and peeresses' and 'baronets' with average rentals of £8,000 and £3,000, have 12 per cent of the total land, while his two classes of freeholders between them collar 59 per cent of the total – nevertheless the fact that they could be seriously advanced by a most conscientious political economist does indicate that, as far as aggregate statistics will take us, a stability thesis for the eighteenth-century peasantry would be just as plausible as the decline thesis.

At this point, however, the lures and snares of fanciful statistical speculation must yield to the requirements of more solid argument about the behaviour of the land market. For in all this discussion of the structure of landownership the implicit assumption has been that the important factor is the distribution by estate sizes, and that any particular pattern of distribution might be produced by widely different velocities of transfers between individuals. Nevertheless, a profound change in the character of the land market has been adduced as one of the major factors, on the demand side, in explaining a decline in the peasantry between 1660 and 1740. It was also adduced, incidentally, to explain a decline in the gentry in the same period; but the statistical evidence for any such decline now seems to be rather thin – in effect, the decline of existing gentry was just about balanced by the emergence of new gentry.[1]

The consistency and cogency of the Habakkuk logic does seem to be open to some doubt. If the English peasantry were forced to sell, during the eighty-odd years after 1660, then they would seem to have caved in

[1] H. J. Habakkuk, 'La disparition du paysan anglais', p. 659; and see F. M. L. Thompson, *English Landed Society in the Nineteenth Century* (1963) pp. 122–7.

before the pressure of low prices and falling incomes, and the burden of taxation, with greater spinelessness than the peasantry of any other European country about which we think we know anything. On the whole, ability to tighten belts beyond any rational starvation point, and stubbornness in hanging on to the family's holding, are two prime peasant characteristics. In addition, it is generally thought that along with this stubbornness the largely subsistence nature of peasant farming enabled peasant farmers to weather times of agricultural adversity rather better than tenant farmers with like-sized holdings, since the peasants were more able to retreat into their shells and insulate themselves from the market. This, at least, would be my reading of the experience of most of the European peasantry in nineteenth-century agricultural depressions. In other words, I would suppose that in order to make any significant fraction of the peasant group into voluntary sellers a quite monumentally severe set of economic pressures would be required, and I do not see that these existed in the relevant period. On the other hand, severe demographic pressures could conceivably be biassed against the peasants in their effects, in that sudden waves of deaths might hit all farmers indifferently, but that while dead tenants would be replaceable by outside recruitment, some dead peasants might leave no successors or successors so weakly attached to their inheritance as to be willing to listen to offers to purchase. One can say no more than that maybe some fortuitous decline in the relative position of the peasant group could have been a consequence of the demographic crises and savage death-rates of, for example, 1665 or 1709–10.

On the other side of the Habakkuk argument, the notion that a drying-up of land supplies obliged would-be purchasers to switch their attention to peasant properties seems to need some clarification.[1] It is quite true that the supply of ready-made gentry or magnate estates coming into the market dwindled, as compared with the 1540–1640 period, as the crown and monastic estates were all absorbed into private ownership, and as the new family legal arrangements of the post-Restoration period, the strict settlements, began to produce their intended effect of keeping family estates inviolate over the generations. But on the other hand, as Habakkuk points out, the demand for these ready-made estates also diminished, for the security-demand for landed

[1] H. J. Habakkuk, 'La disparition du paysan anglais', p. 660; and H. J. Habakkuk, 'The English Land Market in the Eighteenth Century', in J. S. Bromley and E. H. Kossmann (eds.), *Britain and the Netherlands* (1960) pp. 170–1.

investments, which had once led successful mercantile and professional men to place virtually their entire savings in land, was much diminished by the rise first of all of the mortgage as a reliable form of security and then by the growth of the Funds, so that by the early eighteenth century the demand for land had tended to reduce itself to a prestige-demand. Now whether or not the supply and the demand gracefully subsided in tune with one another may be open to question, but it would certainly be unrealistic to suppose that an unabated level of demand was forced to unleash itself on peasant lands. The behaviour of land prices, for what it is worth, would suggest some overall tendency for demand to exceed supply between 1660 and 1760. But the rise from say eighteen years' purchase to say twenty-five years' was not very large, and in any event some part of the rise should be attributed to land prices beginning to follow long-term movements in the rate of interest on the Funds rather than lead them. In all, this evidence would not suggest that excess demand was at all large or insistent, unless, once again, one is to suppose that a small rise in land prices was enough to tempt large numbers of peasants into the market, thus satisfying demand at a slow advance in price. This again would be bound to lead one to conclude that English peasants had previously ceased to behave and act like peasants; and if that was so, if they were already sensitively attuned to market opportunities, then it ceases to be of much importance to the rest of the economy whether they disappeared or not.

The behaviour of the land market has thus far been considered mainly in its bearing on the peasantry. It has also been invoked, in relation to the wealthier classes, as a sort of negative factor in industrialization. This particular model postulates a steady propensity of fortunes accumulated in trade and industry to seek investment for status reasons in gentry-type estates, with the consequence that funds are withdrawn from productive employment for this purpose and the growth of real capital in individual enterprises is thus frustrated. A drying-up of the supply of estates for sale is then introduced as a move which interrupted this flow of savings, and which reluctantly obliged a set of irritated and frustrated businessmen to continue to plough back their savings into their businesses, to the evident benefit of output and the economy at large. Unbeknown to themselves the – presumably selfish – land-hoarding of existing landowners and the unsatisfied land-hunger of *nouveaux riches* produced the beneficent results of preventing the sterilization of savings and forcing them into productive employments.[1]

[1] M. W. Flinn, *Origins of the Industrial Revolution* (1966), p. 46.

No mechanism for ensuring the harmony of divergent interests could be more beautiful, no model more satisfying; but perfect as it may be, we must ask whether this model would actually run, or whether it only exists on the drawing-board. It is said to have functioned in the second half of the eighteenth century, and thus to have made an important or perhaps critical contribution to effective capital accumulation in the decisive period of industrial growth. The actual evidence for a drying-up of the land market is, however, somewhat vague for use as a precision instrument. It consists of a general statement by Mingay that in the eighteenth century as a whole 'the general level of land sales in peace years was much lower than in the sixteenth and seventeenth centuries'; and a slightly more restricted conclusion that 'the inflow of new families into the ranks of landowners was much lower between the 1730s and the end of the eighteenth century than in the previous two hundred years'.[1] Neither of these circumspect generalizations would appear to be designed to bear the weight of arguments requiring important effects to have been produced in a limited period – the second half, or last quarter, of the eighteenth century – and moreover requiring these effects to come from movements on the supply side of the land market. Though Mingay, following Habakkuk, undoubtedly means to argue that the supply did dwindle, because of the cessation of major land market upheavals on the scale of the dissolution of the monasteries and the Civil War, and because of the effectiveness of strict settlements, his conclusions are also compatible with a drying-up of demand because of the development of substitutes for land as a security-investment.

The evidence that a drying-up of the land market did occur does not, at present, seem to be at all conclusive. Against the evidence presented by Habakkuk, on which Mingay relies, that in the first half of the eighteenth century the number of final concords (used in conveyancing) and of private estate acts was significantly lower than previously, we have to set the evidence about the behaviour of sales by auction and of private estate acts in the second half of the eighteenth century.[2] This shows, firstly, that sales by auction increased almost without pause from 1778 until 1811, the only years in which total sales were lower than in the preceding year being 1785, 1789 and 1790, 1794, 1797 and 1798, and 1804. Admittedly this rising trend does not necessarily mean that total

[1] G. E. Mingay, *English Landed Society in the Eighteenth Century* (1963) p. 39.

[2] H. J. Habakkuk, 'The English Land Market in the Eighteenth Century', pp. 155–7; F. M. L. Thompson, 'The Land Market in the Nineteenth Century', *Oxford Econ. Papers*, IX (1957) pp. 285–9; and his *English Landed Society*, p. 214.

land sales were rising, since sale by auction was a comparatively novel selling device when the tax was imposed on it in 1778, and it could be that the subsequent rise in the volume auctioned reflected only a secular trend in the popularization of the new method at the expense of older methods of private sale. Secondly, the annual flow of private estate acts, which had been declining, turned upward from 1760 and entered a rising trend until 1814, interrupted by a pronounced depression – virtually a complete stagnation – only in the decade of the American War, which is also known to have witnessed a general depression in such forms of domestic investment as canals, turnpikes and enclosures.

These two indicators are not conclusive for a view that the volume of land sales was increasing in the second half of the eighteenth century. But if we look at what was apparently happening to land prices, we must at least regard very sceptically any idea that the volume of land sales was actually declining because of a withholding of supply. The only guide we have to the movement of land prices in this period is a table of numbers of years' purchase produced by Arthur Young in 1812.[1] It is doubtless a great deal less accurate than its air of precision implies; but its direction of movement seems credible, and it must suffice until some modern research is carried out on land prices. It shows that the price was 32 years' purchase in 1768–73, fell to $23\frac{1}{4}$ years in 1778–89 during the American War and its aftermath, rose again to 27 years in 1792–9, and to 28 years in 1805–11. By no stretch of the imagination is this a run of prices indicative of an unslaked and frustrated demand and a niggardly supply; on the contrary, if anything it shows demand-determined prices, in the sense that weakness of demand in the uncertain atmosphere of the 1778–89 decade seems the most likely internal cause of a low price, which would then reflect an overstocked market. But leaving the shorter-period fluctuations aside, the general level of these prices bears no comparison with periods of real shortage of properties in the market, such as the 1860s, when prices of 40–65 years' purchase were not uncommon. It is interesting to note that the actual purchasers, at these 1860 levels, were rather more likely to be *nouveaux riches* from trade and industry than to be established landowners.[2]

If, therefore, we must doubt the existence of the phenomenon, we

[1] Arthur Young, *An Enquiry into the Progressive Value of Money in England* (1812).

[2] F. M. L. Thompson, unpublished D.Phil. thesis, Oxford, 1956, 'The Economic and Social Background of the English Landed Interest, 1840–70', Chap. IV.

must also ask for a fuller explanation of the working of the mechanism and a more complete description of its moving parts. For even if we grant for the sake of argument that in the long view land transfers were less active in the eighteenth century than in the sixteenth and seventeenth, and that this change may have had important economic effects, we need to know much more about the likely nature of those effects and the means by which they might have been produced. The theory of demand-frustration requires some sort of explanation of the duration of the frustration. If we were dealing not with a case of hope deferred but with a postponement of demand for landed status so prolonged that it eventually led to a complete abandonment of the ambition, then we would certainly be in the presence of a profound change in social attitudes and aspirations, of a type which we would expect to produce profound long-term shifts in economic structure and activity. For if the ambition to found a landed family ceased to be part of the motivation and way of life of even a sizeable fraction of the wealthier members of the commercial, professional and industrial classes, then many important economic, social and political consequences might be expected to follow. Any pronounced swelling of the proportion of the wealthy classes which was content to remain indefinitely non-landed should have led to a very great rise in the volume of savings retained within non-landed enterprises – as a wild guess, one could claim that the annual turnover of the land market in the 1780–1815 period was of the order of 50 per cent of annual domestic fixed capital formation. It should have led to a great increase in entrepreneurial drive and initiative, since such people would tend to concentrate whole-heartedly, and generation after generation, on their businesses, and would tend not to keep looking over their shoulders at the landed gentry. It should have led to a great increase in the number of very wealthy who were permanent city residents, with repercussions on the intensity and quality of civic pride and civic activity. And it should have led to the growth of an independent group of the very wealthy, which, having no ties with the landed aristocracy and gentry, should have acted as an effective political counterbalance to them.

Now it may be argued that all these things did happen in some degree, during the nineteenth century; and it thus becomes a matter of individual judgement as to whether they happened in such a pronounced degree as to make such a causal relationship probable. At present, however, I would argue firstly, that it had never been the case that all wealth accumulated outside agriculture had sought landed status, so

52

that the existence of some contentedly non-landed wealthy men in the nineteenth century was not necessarily a new factor. And secondly, that the evidence shows a very steady tendency of men with large fortunes gained in industry, finance, commerce and the professions to deck themselves out with landed estates. Landed status and a country life has, of course, not ceased to exercise its attractions to this day, and the country mansions and sporting estates acquired by the property developers with some of the proceeds of the bonanza of the later 1950s are well known. But if there has been any modern tendency for a decline in the propensity of this sort of wealth to go into real estate, I would argue that it did not become apparent any earlier than the 1880s, and did so then principally because of great and justified uncertainty as to the long-term prospects for land values.[1]

The argument is of course inconclusive, since the existence of the well-known estate-purchasers from the ranks of industry or banking in the nineteenth century – the Arkwrights, Peels, Marshalls, Barings Loyds, Brasseys, Cunliffe-Listers, Courtaulds and so on – does not prove that the ambition or habit of estate-building had not died out among some other group of industrialists, bankers and merchants. But if it be conceded that this sort of nominal roll suggests that the alleged demand-frustration might have been more a case of hope deferred than one of hope abandoned, then our model would appear to be faced with some running-in problems. For if the image is that of a successful businessman who wanted to put his fortune, or a slice of it, into landed estate, but being momentarily unable to do so because of scarcity of properties for sale then bided his time until a suitable property did come on the market, the question arises of what he did with his funds while he was waiting. The model requires that he should plough them back into further expansion of his business. But common sense would be just as likely to dictate that if a sufficient fortune had already been accumulated either it, or any subsequent savings, should be put aside in some more liquid assets than plant, machinery and goodwill; for the assumption is, in this situation, that the businessman is waiting for something suitable to come into the market, and he cannot predict when this will be, and whether that moment will be a good moment for him to realize his trading assets. Therefore the savings released for more productive uses by inability to make land purchases might easily be steered into alternative uses which were little, if at all, more productive than landownership, such as the Funds – or even lending on mortgages, which would enable

[1] F. M. L. Thompson, *English Landed Society*, pp. 318–20.

E

the landowners to postpone a little longer the sale of the estates which the lender was apparently anxious to buy.

In any case, the drying-up of the supply of estates for sale is said to have stemmed, in part, from the increasing ability of established land-owners to go on borrowing without being forced to sell; so that the ratio of indebtedness to annual income seems to have risen markedly during the eighteenth century, while at the same time forced sales by debt-ridden landowners, which had been common in the seventeenth century, became quite rare.[1] This development was caused in part by the perfection of legal devices – the strict settlement, which permitted long-term mortgages to be raised for specified family purposes, or at the moments of resettlement; and the mortgage itself, where the development of the equity of redemption provided security to both borrower and lender. But it was caused, in even greater part, by the growth of credit available for this sort of lending. Some of this was institutional; some of the London private banks made considerable advances on mortgage or bond to landowners, and presumably the expanding insurance offices of the eighteenth century also lent on mortgage. But much of it, as far as one can tell easily the major part, was private lending. All manner of people might lend on mortgage in the eighteenth century, and as much of the business was channelled through attorneys the individual lenders often remain very anonymous figures. But it is extremely probable that many of the private lenders were from that class of businessmen which in earlier centuries would have been land-purchasers. These men went on lending to landowners when they must have known that, in Habakkuk's words, most borrowing by landowners was for non-productive purposes.[2] That is, the borrowing was mainly for such things as the funding of short-term debts to tradesmen, or gambling debts, the financing of personal extravagance, or the financing of the younger members of the family; there was no great likelihood that the loans would be used to improve the income-producing capacity of the estate and thus make it more viable. Hence the lenders must have known that if they refused to make advances they would be helping to ensure that sooner or later the already indebted landowners would be forced to sell; and since the lenders are alleged to have been people who wanted to buy estates, this would have been their logical course of action. That they did nothing of the sort, but continued to behave as willing lenders on mortgages, surely tends to show that if there was a switch in the destination of mercantile

---

[1] H. J. Habakkuk, 'The English Land Market . . .', pp. 158–60, 164–5.
[2] Ibid., p. 164.

savings, it was not a switch from unproductive uses (land purchase) to productive uses (industrial investment), but rather a switch from one form of unproductive use (land purchase) to another form of unproductive use (supporting existing landowners). In other words, there was little transformation of fixed-interest capital into risk-capital; but a form of near-fixed-interest capital, which had had its imperfections since when it had gone into land it had been subject to all the uncertainties of rent movements and estate management, had simply become a more perfect form of fixed-interest capital, returning its steady $3\frac{1}{2}$ or 5 per cent or whatever it might be and occasioning virtually no bother to the lender. The very minor point, that there were very few 'new' industrialists either among the mortgagees or among the land-purchasers of the second half or the last quarter of the eighteenth century, may be most easily explained by the obvious fact that 'new' industrialists were at this time rather small fry, and by and large did not yet have fortunes of the size to seek either of these outlets. In other words, they were still on the make; when they had made, there is no convincing evidence that they were land-shy.

The general direction of the argument so far has perhaps appeared wantonly destructive, though I would plead that its purpose has been to show that it is difficult to credit either the structure of landownership or the behaviour of the land market with any very direct, positive or dynamic role in the critical period of English economic growth. Rather, those aspects which I have been examining would appear to be derivative. It may be, however, that we have all been looking in the wrong places for the positive and dynamic contributions of the landed system to economic growth. Firstly, the whole business of wealth going into landed status has largely been regarded in the light of good productive capital running away into the sands and dissipating its potential expansive force. Even if, as was sometimes but not necessarily the case, the newly landed turned out to be more efficient and progressive estate managers than the older gentry they replaced, such a study as E. L. Jones's of the Arkwrights shows the retarding and inhibiting effects which a withdrawal of capital from industry might have on the industry.[1] This, however, might be no more than the necessary price which the economy had to pay for having any expansion. For the question of motivation is involved, and though I would not wish to pontificate on

[1] E. L. Jones, 'Industrial Capital and Landed Investment: the Arkwrights in Herefordshire, 1809–43', in E. L. Jones and G. E. Mingay, *Land, Labour and Population in the Industrial Revolution.*

the motives of businessmen, it seems possible that the drive to acquire a fortune was kept going by a drive to acquire status. In the particular environment of eighteenth- and nineteenth-century England political and social attitudes conferred the highest status on the landed classes, and the structure of landownership, the attitudes of the established landowners, and the machinery of the land market all served to make it possible to make at least a start on acquiring this status by accumulation and purchase. In a different society, with different political and social attitudes and institutions, high status may attach to different possessions, and as long as they can be acquired by purchase they may supply an equally potent social motivation for business enterprise. But the English landed system, though by no means the only possible system for encouraging the accumulation of fortunes, was at least sufficiently flexible and sufficiently open to newcomers to be capable of imparting this essential ingredient of purpose to entrepreneurs. It helped to call forth enterprise; and by its very existence it helped, once ambition was satisfied, to distort and dampen down the further course of enterprise. But we should not complain of the restrictive effects of the golf-course-shooting-country-house syndrome in inculcating amateurish and lethargic management in, for example, the late nineteenth century, without recalling the expansive effects of the same features in keeping the acquisitive spirit energetically alive.

Secondly, the unproductive character of the operations of the land market has probably been overdone. Even if we discount the possibility that new landowners from trade or industry imparted an upward twist to agricultural productivity, and even if we were to admit that the land purchasers were withdrawing capital from highly productive employment, it still remains true that no consideration has ever been given to what happened on the other side of the capital-transfer equation. When estates were bought, the sellers were put in funds; no one seems to have asked what they then did with them. In only a few cases, and those mainly mid-nineteenth-century ones, have I discovered a seller using the proceeds for productive investment in the remainder of his estate. The general case, no doubt, was for the proceeds to be used in discharging debts; but the creditors, being thus put in funds, were enabled to extend new credit to someone. Maybe they used these opportunities unworthily, merely to extend further loans to other worthless landowners; but maybe they then gave credit elsewhere, perhaps they helped to finance the purchaser of the mill which its owner was selling in order to pay off his creditor. The ways of credit are wonderful; some are circular, some help to fertilize productive projects. It would be unwise to assume that the sums which changed hands through the land market were in some way 'lost' to the economy.

Thirdly, if we look at the behaviour of landowners as producers and consumers, which is the second general item on my original agenda, I think it can be argued that the greater stability of the eighteenth century induced some significant changes. I am not thinking of the instances of entrepreneurial activities by landowners in such things as coal-mining and iron-making, which are well known but whose general importance is difficult to assess. Rather, it may be that the expectation of family and estate continuity, engendered by the security against dissipation provided by the strict settlement, was an important factor in inducing a numerous body of landowners to take that long-term view of prospects which is a necessary part of readiness to engage their capital in such investments as canals, turnpikes and enclosures. Enhanced confidence in the future of the family as a landed family would also seem important in causing a change in landowners' consumption habits. It would seem possible that the relative insecurity of the seventeenth century caused landowners to spend their surplus income either on riotously extravagant current consumption of luxuries or on durables of high liquidity like gold and jewellery. Greater confidence could have caused a switch towards conspicuous investment. Whatever Flinn may say about a stagnation of stately home building between the 1730s and the 1790s, the eighteenth century will continue to retain its image as a century of extremely wide-spread building of country houses and mansions until it is demolished by serious research.[1] A glance at Colvin's *Dictionary of Architects* should serve to counteract Flinn's glance at six of Pevsner's volumes on the *Buildings of England*, in removing the impression that sixty years of the eighteenth century saw little such building.

Now, in economic terms, this building activity is usually dismissed as either 'conspicuous investment' or as 'capital consumption'. In comparison with what these landowners had been doing – or, rather, not doing – earlier, neither of these labels seems particularly helpful. In fact, the construction of country houses was an investment activity with multiplier effects in creating employment for builders, quarry-workers, brick-makers, the furniture and the furnishing trades, and so on, and moreover creating it on a country-wide basis. It was accompanied by the building of town houses by many of the great and of the gentry, not merely in London, but also in many provincial towns which thus

[1] M. W. Flinn, *Origins of the Industrial Revolution*, p. 48.

acquired their Georgian town centres. Moreover, there were certain forward linkages as well, since once built the new and larger houses provided increased employment for domestic servants and outdoor staffs. The effects on the rest of the economy may not have been as great as the effects of a similar amount of investment in other and less sumptuous construction would have been. That, however, is scarcely the point. The point is that the social system had already provided for enormous inequalities in the distribution of incomes and wealth; within that given context, it was a great deal more stimulating for the rest of the economy that landowners should have spent some of their incomes in this extravagant type of investment, than that they should have spent their entire incomes on wines and silks.

Far from having been, from this point of view, ushered in by a cessation of country-house building, the Industrial Revolution may well have been ushered in by a spate of such building. For the growth of consumer demand, of the home market, is now reaching the height of its influence as a general explanation of economic growth in the eighteenth century. It is in this context that the contribution of agricultural change in the first half of the eighteenth century is now most firmly set.

It is this factor which Eversley has recently carried forward from 1750 to 1780, and implicitly beyond.[1] Country-house building must have stimulated this demand, but to what extent, and with what importance relative to other stimulants, we could not tell until a great deal of measurement has been done.

Finally, it is perhaps in this sphere that the third item on my agenda, the derived effects of the landed system, were of greatest importance. To make only two points, we should consider from the point of view of their role in the home market two groups which owed their existence to the landed system: the younger sons of the landowners, particularly of the great landowners; and the tenant farmers. From the point of view of really productive employment, the role of the younger sons has frequently been exaggerated: they did not flock into the counting-houses so much as into the army, the navy and the Church. But perhaps they did not flock anywhere at all so much as into that leisured class of 20,000 'gentlemen and ladies living on incomes' which Colquhoun identified in 1801, and whom he defined as 'persons having colonial and East India

[1] D. E. C. Eversley, 'The Home Market and Economic Growth in England, 1750–1780', in E. L. Jones and G. E. Mingay, Land, *Labour and Population in the Industrial Revolution*.

property, funds, and jointures, &c. including foreign incomes'.[1] This idle crew, living on their unearned incomes, were, he thought, injecting £14 million a year of purchasing power into the economy. Of course not all of this group were recipients of jointure or portion income derived from landed estates; but certainly some fraction of it did represent the way in which the landed system, having aggregated incomes from land nominally into the hands of relatively few landlords, then proceeded to distribute this income among a larger number of people. It must, of course, also be doubtful whether Eversley would admit this group to his key class of 'middling consumers', or whether he would firmly place them in the opulent class who were 'luxury consumers' and whose expenditure patterns were not important in creating the demand for manufactures. Colquhoun, however, put them on an average income of £700 per family, making them slightly less wealthy than his class of manufacturers.

There can be much less doubt that a fair proportion of the class of tenant farmers came into Eversley's group of 'middling consumers'. Colquhoun reckoned that there were 160,000 of them with average incomes of £120, exactly on a par in income terms with the lesser clergy and dissenting ministers, slightly more affluent than the innkeepers, slightly less well off than naval and military officers, or shopkeepers. With their families, the farmers would at this rate have formed about one-third of Eversley's middle classes. There is no means of checking the accuracy of Colquhoun's figures, but they receive some confirmation from the fact that the total number of cultivators (with holdings worth £50 a year or more), including in their number swarms of weavers and other non-farmers who had holdings, was far greater than this, some 590,000 of them appearing in the income-tax returns for 1812.[2] Hence Colquhoun may at least be held to have succeeded in excluding those who did not really depend on farming for their living, and perhaps in also excluding a number who did, but who were very small holders. On the other hand, only 62,000 farmers appear as having holdings worth £150 a year or more in 1812, so that Colquhoun may have pitched his average income on the high side. Without, therefore, committing ourselves to the view that the farmers did form one-third of the middle classes, we may still hold that very many farmers were indeed in that social and economic category, and we need only remember some of

[1] Patrick Colquhoun, *Treatise on Indigence*, pp. 23–4.
[2] P. K. O'Brien, 'British Incomes and Property in the early Nineteenth Century', *Econ. Hist. Rev.*, 2nd ser., XII (1960) p. 263.

Cobbett's fulminations over the wasteful extravagance of farmers' domestic furnishings and fittings, not to mention their wives' and daughters' clothing, to conclude that they had indeed developed the middle-class spending habits which are the key element in Eversley's model. It would seem possible, moreover, that a higher proportion of farmers' incomes might be available for expenditure on the manufactured goods of the expanding industries than was the case with some of the town-dwelling non-agricultural middle class, since farmers had much lower food expenditures, and in effect no expenditures at all on housing.

This group of tenant farmers had undoubtedly expanded in size since 1688; for by 1808 the income-tax returns show that 83 per cent of the farmland was occupied by tenants, whereas in 1688 it was probably only between 60 and 70 per cent at the most. It was also a group which had probably only learnt to dispense with household production of many of its consumer goods in the course of the eighteenth century, so that the net addition to the total home demand for the products of manufacturing industry was likely to have been much greater than the simple growth in numbers or in individual incomes alone would imply. It may turn out that the landed system made its most decisive contribution to economic growth first by creating a large body of tenant farmers, and then by sustaining and increasing its relative importance in the eighteenth century, forcing or encouraging these tenants to adopt an increasingly commercial outlook and enabling them to command respectable middling-sized incomes. It thus provided a framework which funnelled part of the proceeds of agricultural growth into the hands of farmers who did not hoard or try to add parcel to parcel of their holdings as peasants might do, but who spent reasonably freely on manufactured articles, gee-gaws and fripperies – the things whose production the Industrial Revolution was all about.

1. *Diagrammatic representation of hand reaping (1844)*. The reaper clutched a handful of straw in the left hand, while at the same time drawing the tool towards him in a cutting (reap hook) or sawing (sickle) action, as near to and parallel with the ground as possible. Handfuls of cut straw were then laid on to ready prepared bands. In this illustration the reapers are organized three to a ridge with a bandster servicing two ridges.

2. *Bagging with the broad hook and stick*. The usual practice was to cut forwards alongside the standing crop. Two followers were usually employed to bind and stook.

3. *Mowing with the Flemish scythe and 'pik'.* Known in Flanders since the 15th century, attempts to popularize it in Britain met with little success. Tensioned by the 'pik' the corn was cut by a series of swinging strokes, the harvester advancing directly into the crop cutting half a sheaf on each side of him.

4. *Diagrammatic representation of the mowing operation (1844),* showing (left to right) the three scythe types—cradle scythe with S-shaped sned, poled scythe and Y-shaped scythe, and the four ancillary operations—gathering (c), raking (h), binding (e) and stooking (f).

3 Labour supply and demand in European agriculture 1800–1880[1]

E. J. T. COLLINS

Until quite recent times the majority of tasks on western European farms have been performed using labour-intensive methods. Even so, historians have seldom examined in depth the role of labour as a factor of production in agriculture. Interest in the human agent has centred largely on his social and political condition and enthusiasm for farm technology has been chiefly confined to the study of labour-saving machinery. Thus while the machine is often ranked as the chief techno-logical indicator of agricultural progress, so it has been generally assumed that there existed in European agriculture no real demand for labour-saving until relatively late on in the nineteenth century, when in the more economically advanced countries mechanization began to displace hand-tool processes.

It can be argued, though, that the real problems of nineteenth-century western European agricultures were far from exclusively those con-cerned with under-employment and low labour productivity. An impor-tant, and in the final analysis perhaps the chief limiting factor in increased farm output was the capacity of the farm labour force at times of work bottlenecks. Even in the most lowly productive agricultures and under conditions of chronic structural unemployment the highly seasonal nature of crop production can easily create serious labour shortages at peak activity periods of the farming year.

Summer labour requirements in western European agricultures increased rapidly and continuously throughout the period 1800–80, first as the area under cultivation expanded and subsequently as

[1] I am indebted to Dr E. L. Jones for helpful criticism of earlier drafts of this paper. I wish to thank Professor C. Tyler for help with the literature on Germany. A forthcoming paper, E. J. T. Collins, 'Harvest Technology and Labour Supply in Britain, 1790–1870', *Econ. Hist. Rev.* (December 1969) and the earlier paper by E. L. Jones, 'The Agricultural Labour Market in England, 1793–1872', *Econ. Hist. Rev.*, 2nd ser., XVII (1964) pp. 322–38, should be referred to for otherwise undocumented British experiences mentioned below.

mixed-farming systems became more intensive, as off-farm fertilizers and feeding-stuffs came into use and as technologies became more recognizably land-saving. On an increasing scale corn, root and leguminous crops with their overlapping work schedules competed with each other for supplies of summer labour. This bias of western European agriculture towards products and processes needing large inputs of manual labour rendered it particularly vulnerable to any deterioration of the farm labour market during the summer months such as inevitably took place during the early industrial phase of economic growth, when labour began to leave the land and when farm populations stabilized and then declined. The observed tendency was for industry and agriculture to expand together and to compete increasingly within the same market for supplies of labour. Initially western European agricultures coped with the drain on their peak-season workforces by complex redistributions of labour and by subtle and unmechanical technologies.

I

Historically the small grains harvest has been the main farm operation to create an exceptional demand for labour, fully draining the local pool and perhaps requiring substantial imports of migrant workers. The grain harvest was a critical operation, firstly because timely performance was essential if heavy crop losses through the shedding of overripe grain or the spoilage of damp, badly laid grain were to be avoided, and secondly because harvest labour requirements could fluctuate by as much as 50 per cent from season to season, which made necessary not only a large but also an extremely elastic supply of labour. The greatest danger was rapid and convergent crop ripening which created a simultaneous demand for labour over a wide area and seriously disrupted inter-regional labour flows which under normal conditions were able to exploit the different timings of the harvest between upland and lowland, heavy land and light land and hence satisfy most local demands.

There is overwhelming evidence that in nineteenth-century Europe grain production tended to grow much faster than supplies of harvest labour. Cropping and yield data for Britain during the first half of the nineteenth century are notoriously inadequate, but we can suppose that total grain production (in England and Wales) increased by 45–55 per cent between 1800 and 1850, with perhaps the fastest rate of increase occurring between 1835 and 1855 when on a more or less stable area crop yields improved substantially. Between 1855 and 1875 output levelled off and in some areas, notably in the north and west, output probably declined.[1]

Between 1800 and 1850 grain output in France and Germany expanded at least as rapidly as in Britain and continued to expand throughout the third quarter of the century.

TABLE I

Total Grain Production in France and Germany[2]

France (1803-12 = 100)		Germany (1816 = 100)	
1803-12	100		
1815-24	108	1816	100
1825-34	121		
1835-44	137		
1845-54	155	1846-55	145
1855-64	166	1856-65	169
1865-74	173	1866-75	191
1875-84	175	1876-85	208

Thus in France output increased by 55 per cent between 1803-15 and 1845-54, and by a further 13 per cent between 1845-54 and 1875-84. In Germany, where area expansion was greater and yield improvements occurred later (in the 1860s), output increased by about 45 per cent between 1816 and 1846-55 and by 43 per cent between 1846-55 and 1876-85.

The increase in harvest labour requirements (assuming constant techniques and a direct correlation between corn output and labour input)

[1] Nineteenth-century changes in crop yields are summarized in P. G. Craigie, 'Statistics of Agricultural Production', *Journal of the Statistical Society*, XLVI (1883) pp. 1–47. See also M. J. R. Healy and E. L. Jones, 'Wheat Yields in England, 1815–1859', *Journal of the Royal Statistical Society*, Ser. A, 125 (1962) pp. 574–9; L. Drescher, 'The Development of Agricultural Production in Great Britain and Ireland from the early nineteenth century', *Manchester School*, XXIII (1955) p. 167.

[2] Production data for France (wheat, barley, oats, rye) from J. C. Toutain, *Le Produit de l'Agriculture Française de 1700 à 1958* (I.S.E.A., Paris, 1961) pt. II, p. 16; and for Germany (wheat, barley, oats, rye, spelt, mixed corn, buckwheat) from W. G. Hoffmann, *Das Wachstum der Deutschen Wirtschaft seit der Mitte des 19. Jahrhunderts* (Berlin, 1965) pp. 271–94. The 1816 datum is an extrapolation based on Finckenstein and Bittermann's area data summarized in W. G. Hoffmann, 'The Take-off in Germany', in W. W. Rostow (ed.), *The Economics of Take-off into Sustained Growth* (1963) pp. 101–3.

would in practice have been rather higher than the grain output figures suggest. Over most of western Europe, but in Britain and France particularly, the major product growth occurred in wheat whose labour requirements, according to type of tool employed, were between 20 per cent (sickle) and 100 per cent (scythe) greater than for barley and oats.[1] In addition, more extensive cultivations of root and fodder crops, whose work schedules often overlapped on to both ends of the harvest, would have had the effect of increasing the demand for workers over a more compressed harvesting period.[2]

Nineteenth-century occupational statistics are too imprecise to allow more than very crude approximations of long-run changes in labour-supply schedules. It is notoriously difficult to ascertain just what part of the total population should be described as agricultural, and what part of the agricultural population should be described as 'active'. In the pre-industrial and proto-industrial economies the 'two sector' model is an inconvenient tool for analysis of the physical integration of agriculture and industry; and the highly complex seasonal exchanges of labour between different sectors of the economy renders it extremely difficult to discover the exact size of the farm labour force during the summer months and during the harvest in particular. It is clear nevertheless that over the greater part of the nineteenth century there existed growing disparities between harvest work demand and harvest labour supply. In Britain the official agricultural labour force is estimated to have increased by 24 per cent between 1801 and 1851 while crop demand grew by over 50 per cent, and to have fallen by 15–20 per cent between 1851 and 1871, with crop demand remaining more or less constant. Hoffmann has calculated that between 1816 and 1861 the German agricultural labour force grew by 23 per cent and crop demand by at least 60 per cent.[3] Between 1850 and 1880 the gap became wider as rural population growth slowed down and crop demand increased by over 50 per cent. The French situation can be quantified rather better.

Table II shows a continuous deterioration in grain output/labour supply ratios, after 1815-24. Toutain suggests that over the period 1803-12–1865-74 the total 'active' (male and female) agricultural work-

---

[1] In France, for example, the wheat area grew from 4·592 million hectares in 1815 to 6·947 million hectares in 1875. Toutain, op. cit., pp. 105–7.

[2] Contemporary estimates (for what they are worth) suggest that the fodder crop area in England and Wales more than doubled between 1812 and 1854, Dreschner, loc. cit., p. 167. German sugar-beet production increased from 2·33 million to 4·738 million metric tons between 1846 and 1880, Hoffmann, op. cit., pp. 284–5.   [3] Hoffmann, loc. cit., p. 103.

force grew by only 20–25 per cent compared with a 60 per cent growth in grain production.

The harvest-field situation was much more complex than simple enumeration of farm population heads suggests. Harvest workforces were composed not only of full-time farm workers but also of large numbers of women, children, old people, tramps, tradesmen, industrial workers and migrant labourers, each with their different supply curve. The extreme complexity of inter- and intra-sectoral labour flows at harvest-time renders it possible to explore long-run changes in harvest labour supply schedules only at the most impressionistic levels.

TABLE II

Harvest Labour Requirements and Farm Labour Supply in France, 1803–1884[1]

(**1803-12** = 100)

	Total grain output	Total agricultural population	Male population active in agriculture
1803-12	100	100	100
1815-24	108	101	105
1825-34	121	102	109
1835-44	137	104	114
1845-54	155	105	120
1855-64	166	107	120
1865-74	173	99	120
1875-84	175	98	125

All evidence suggests that in the industrializing economy the harvest labour force grew more slowly or declined faster than the full-time farm labour force. This relative decline was already apparent before 1850. For it was farm workers, and usually the best farm workers, rather than farmers and part-time farmers who left the land. This exodus was invariably headed by the younger and most highly productive members of the working community. Significantly in France, the *journalier*, day-worker, class declined from the early 1860s, even though the rural population did not reach its official peak until after 1900.[2] We can recognize as well the growing tendency for young agricultural workers

[1] Output data from Toutain, op. cit., p. 16; population data from J. C Toutain, *La Population de la France de 1700 à 1959* (I.S.E.A., Paris, 1963 pp. 48–58, 161, 200–1.

[2] C. P. Kindleberger, *Economic Growth in France and Britain, 1851–1950* (Cambridge, Mass., 1964) p. 215.

to seek non-farm work during the summer months, particularly in years of high economic activity when the demand for unskilled labour in building and construction work was greatest. In mid-Victorian Britain a significant proportion of workers returned as agricultural labourers in the April Census would in August, the harvest month, have been far away in brick-fields, or in ironworks or on building and civil engineering sites. Another important source of loss was the drying-up of many inter-regional migrant labour flows after 1850, the more serious because most migrants took more than one harvest a season and because as piece-workers their work rates were invariably high. In many areas of France and West Germany the deteriorating harvest labour supply position on the larger farms was further aggravated by the fact that as the urban demand for the products of *la Petite Culture* increased, so the small proprietor, the part-time *main d'œuvre*, found it more and more profit-able to spend time cultivating his own holding than to sell his labour to neighbouring farmers.[1]

The decay of rural and cottage industry which for many parts of western Europe had constituted the chief traditional source of casual farm labour was a heavy loss to the harvest-field. In growing urban areas the running-down of cottage looms and spinning-wheels saw the majority of redundants absorbed into factories whose rigid work disciplines destroyed the seasonal work rhythms of the older pre-industrial society. In the more rural areas, the decline initially may have provided agricul-ture with many new recruits, but without improving labour supplies during the harvest, for which operation their labour had previously always been available. In France rural industry contracted more slowly than in Britain or Germany. Even so, large numbers of rural craftsmen had already gone into the factories of Nord and Picardy before 1850. Elsewhere the phenomenon of the peasant industrialist transferring his labour freely between two sectors of the economy had disappeared from most villages by 1900. In Britain, the hand-loom weavers who had once turned out in force to assist with the harvest in the West Riding and Furness, or in East Norfolk and the Cotswolds were no longer available in the 1860s. In the 1830s farmers in southern England had already resigned themselves to the fact that townspeople, and second generation townspeople in particular, were no longer prepared to volunteer their

---

[1] T. E. Cliffe Leslie, 'The Land System of France', in J. W. Probyn (ed.), *Systems of Land Tenure* (new edn, 1881), pp. 306–7, 310. On growth of small-holdings in France after 1850 see J. H. Clapham, *The Economic Development of France and Germany, 1815–1914* (Cambridge, 1921) pp. 160–7.

labour during the harvest. About the same time Irish migrant harvesters were filling the gaps left vacant by colliers, mechanics and textile workers in the Scottish Lowlands. We can be certain too that the Parisian building workers who had harvested during the First Empire did not participate during the Second.[1] A further aggravation was the growing disinclination of women to engage in field work. In the 1860s women still came out from the agricultural townships of the Scottish and English border counties, but their numbers were declining. In other areas the fall-off was rather more serious and farmers were complaining that their non-appearance was a severe set-back to intensive mixed-farming in which efficient and timely performance of summer operations was essential. In Austria in the 1840s there were complaints about the reduced quality of female workers, whose 'fancy notions and yearning after luxuries' led them to prefer Vienna and domestic service to the rigours of field work.[2]

II

The Napoleonic Wars gave western Europe an early taste of harvest labour scarcity. The situation in Britain was probably more acute than on the Continent, for during the period 1793–1815 not only agriculture and the armed forces, but also manufacturing and canal building were competing fiercely within the rural labour market. In some parts of Britain harvesters were already scarce during the first years of the canal boom (1790–2) and by 1794–6 reports of harvest labour forces seriously depleted by navigation works and military service were coming in from most areas of Britain, while in 1793 a Bill was actually introduced into Parliament to prohibit the cutting of canals during the harvest months. There was already an incipient demand for reaping machinery by 1805. In that year an Essex farmer, with his corn 'shelling on the ground for want of cutting', doubted whether there was an agriculturist in the county who thought that 'the invention of a machine for reaping corn would be an injurious discovery'. Before 1800 at least two, and by 1805 a further half-dozen, machine designs had been patented. The deterioration of the harvest labour market during the war years was confirmed by the

---

[1] For the decline of rural industry in France and Germany, see Clapham, op. cit., Chaps. X, XI; Hoffmann, loc. cit., pp. 109–11; H. Sée, *Histoire Économique de la France* (Paris, 1951) pp. 153–75, 295–310; P. Benaerts, *Les Origines de la Grande Industrie Allemande* (Paris, 1933) pp. 373–530 *passim*.

[2] J. Blum, *Noble Landowners and Agriculture in Austria, 1815–1848* (Baltimore, 1948) p. 178.

Wage Inquiry organized by the Board of Agriculture in 1805. This revealed that in England harvest costs stood 54–59 per cent higher, and in Scotland 39–42 per cent higher in 1803 than in 1790, compared with a 6 per cent decrease and a 2 per cent increase in wheat and oat prices. Predictably the rise was greatest in industrial counties (Derbyshire, Lancashire, Northumberland, Nottinghamshire and Yorkshire all returned increases of over 65 per cent) and in counties where the cereal area was rapidly expanding (Cambridge and Lincolnshire both scored over 70 per cent).[1]

In France, harvest labour scarcities appear to have been confined chiefly to the northern departments and to have been most severe in the 1790s. In 1794 only an estimated one-tenth of the usual 20,000–24,000 migrant harvesters came into Meaux, while strikes occurred at Narbonne, and around Paris building workers had to be temporarily drafted into the harvest-fields. In Vendée farmers were able to find neither enough workers nor, because of a temporary interruption of German and Austrian supplies, a sufficient quantity of tools. The Commission d'Agriculture et des Artes could at that stage only recommend frantic local officials in Meaux to arm themselves with scythes and sickles and appeal to the populace through the medium of 'des hymnes patriotiques'.[2] In Germany farmers' complaints about the 'crying evil' of excessive advances in the wages of servants and day labourers were noted by Thaër soon after 1800.[3] Other reports of harvest labour scarcities came from as far away as North Italy and Austria; in the latter country harvest workers were so scarce on one estate that in 1811 circulars were distributed to surrounding villages advertising for hands. In succeeding years this practice was extended to the more distant mountain villages, soldier labour was brought in, while in 1819 local estates banded together in an attempt to stabilize wages and to regularize harvest labour flows.[4]

The two or three decades after Waterloo brought temporary respite.[5]

[1] A. H. John, 'Farming in Wartime: 1793–1815', in E. L. Jones and G. E. Mingay (eds.), *Land, Labour and Population in the Industrial Revolution* (1967) pp. 32–5; *Communications to the Board of Agriculture*, V, pt. I (1806) p. 113; A. Young, *General View . . . Essex*, I (1805), pp. 372–3; see also *Communications to the Board of Agriculture*, V, pt. I (1806) pp. 17–38, 39–121 *passim*.

[2] R. Tresse, 'Le Développement de la Fabrication des Faux en France de 1785 à 1827', *Annales*, X (1955) pp. 354–8.

[3] A. D. Thaër, *Principles of Agriculture*, trans. W. Shaw and C. W. Johnson, I (1855) p. 59.

[4] R. Forsyth, *The Principles and Practice of Agriculture*, II (Edinburgh, 1804), p. 196; Blum, op. cit., pp. 175–7.

[5] J. D. Marshall, *The Old Poor Law, 1795–1834* (1968) pp. 26–7, 35–43; A. Chatelain, 'La Lente Progression de la Faux', *Annales*, XI (1956) pp. 498–9.

Fast-growing rural populations swollen by recruits from declining domestic industries and by increasing numbers of seasonal migrant workers provided farmers with a sufficient supply of labour to satisfy most existing and additional harvest labour demands. The incentives to labour-saving innovation were noticeably weaker than during the war years to the extent that in some of the more labour-flush areas harvests which had previously taken three or four weeks may now have been completed within just a few days. Reports of labour scarcities, all too frequent in wartime, now occurred only very occasionally, usually in rapid crop-ripening years, when the chief complaint was less about physical shortages of labour as such than about marginal increases in its supply price.

The first signs of renewed deterioration of the harvest labour market appeared not as is conventionally assumed in the 1850s, but rather earlier, in the mid-1830s. The 1850s appear in fact to have seen only the resumption of an already well-established trend temporarily interrupted by the European economic crisis of the later 1840s. In Britain, France and Germany the mid-1830s saw a marked upswing in industrial activity which coincided with agricultural revival and the first phase of railway construction to dry up a large part of the conspicuous rural labour surplus.[1] The British situation was summed up by the 1836 Report of the Poor Law Commissioners:

> The price of provisions is still reasonable; the demand for labour in the manufacturing districts unprecedented; railroads are construct-ing in every part of England; the iron founders are all seeking additional hands to keep pace with their enormous orders, and there is an increased desire on the part of the weakened portion of the community to assist their poorer neighbours to seek their fortunes in the colonies.[2]

In 1837 East Anglia reported a considerable exodus of young men to London and the railways. Hoxne in Suffolk, for example, described a 'totally altered spirit. . . . If work is not to be found at home, they [the farm workers] are both ready and anxious to seek it elsewhere'.[3] Rising

---

[1] A. D. Gayer, Rostow and Schwartz, *The Growth and Fluctuation of the British Economy, 1790–1850*, I (Oxford, 1953) pp. 242–76; J. Marczewski, 'The take-off hypothesis and French experience', Rostow, op. cit., Table 10, p. 135; Hoffmann, loc. cit., Graphs 4–6, pp. 107–8.

[2] *Second Annual Report & the Poor Law Commissions* (1836) p. 299.

[3] *15th Report of the Select Committee on the Poor Law Amendment Act* (1838) pp. 21–4. See also Collins, loc. cit.

yields, higher corn acreages and an accelerated movement away from less labour-intensive barley and oats into more labour-intensive wheat increased harvest labour requirements after 1835, with the predictable result that complaints of shedding corn, high wages and too few workers quickly developed.

This striking tendency for agriculture and industry to expand simultaneously was apparent also in France.[1] Marczewski has shown that 1835–44 saw in France the peak growth rate in both the agricultural and industrial product. In France and Germany railway building (5,850 miles of track were completed here between 1830 and 1850) would have had a marked and disruptive influence on many local farm-labour markets. Harvest labour shortages were quick to develop in France; harvest labour requirements grew 15 per cent over the decade 1835–44 while according to Toutain the active male population increased by only 4 per cent. By 1839 it was already impossible in some years to obtain 'at any price' enough workers to secure the crop without loss. Nor in certain areas could farmers confidently rely on the timely appearance of the customary migrant harvesters on whose labour they were so heavily dependent. In 1836 harvest wages in Bouches du Rhône hit an unprecedented 5–6 francs per day with demand still unsatisfied. In some quarters at least the only solution was thought to rest with reaping machinery.

Evidence from central Europe pointed in the same general direction. In Lower Austria the trend towards urbanization intensified after 1830. Between 1831 and 1846, chiefly owing to the growth of Vienna, the population resident in towns of 5,000 and over grew 39 per cent while that in the smaller, chiefly agricultural settlements increased by only 7 per cent. Rural migration, the diversion of many would-be migrant harvesters into railway building and a decline in the female agricultural labour force were chief talking-points among farmers in the mid-1840s. Further east, scarcity of labour was said to be the main constraint on increased agricultural production in Hungary, and as the tillage area increased so the use of the whip and illegal extortions of *Robot* (labour services) from the peasants became the chief instruments of raising the supply.[2]

---

[1] Marczewski, loc. cit., Table 10, p. 135; Toutain, op. cit. (1961) pt. II; Toutain, op. cit. (1963) pp. 200–1; *Journal d'Agriculture Pratique* [hereafter referred to as *JAP*], II, pt. II (1838–9) pp. 44–5. For railway construction in France and Germany, see Benaerts, op. cit., p. 319n.

[2] Blum, op. cit., pp. 172–87.

The third quarter of the nineteenth century saw the critical turning-point in the European farm labour market, as in the proto-industrial economies of the west rural populations stabilized or declined, and as in the agrarian economies of the east and south-east the coming of the railways stimulated the conversion of vast areas of steppe and low-grade pasture into corn land. In western Europe the situation was made worse by a contraction of migrant labour flows, and marked reductions in the supplies of female and part-time industrial workers. The more vigorous uptake of root and fodder crops, and in suburban areas the rapid extension of vegetable and market garden crops, created new and critical elements of on-farm demand for labour during the busy summer months. Farmers soon discovered, if they had not already done so, that the supply of summer labour, and harvest labour in particular, was decidedly inelastic. They discovered too that in a rapidly industrializing economy the farm labour market was increasingly ruled by the trade cycle, that supplies of labour were unpredictable and could fluctuate violently from season to season, and that short-run convergences of crop demand and labour supply schedules could mean an expensive and risky harvest.

The speed with which an apparently overstocked farm labour market could tighten up was brought home to British farmers soon after 1850. In 1851 Caird had described in many areas the 'redundance of labour which oppresses property and depreciates wages', but at the same time he perceived what many others had not, that the over-supply was apt to be exaggerated, and that as men began to withdraw employers would soon discover that the surplus was not as great as they wanted to believe. The inelasticities were already apparent in the harvest of 1852. In 1853, with industry beginning to revive, the *Farmers' Magazine* was bemoaning the effects of the drying-up of the Irish migrant flows, of the 'findings of California' and the 'diggings of Australia' on a labour market which was daily becoming 'more and more the engrossing topic at public and private meetings; the more so probably in agriculture than in any other branch of industry'. The 'event foreseen for some years', a harvest in which really large quantities of grain were lost for want of hands, occurred in 1859. In 1866 it was being forecast, and not for the first time, that farming in the grain-growing districts would be at a discount if 'the difficulty of getting labour at prices compatible with land produce continues'. The early 1870s saw the last major nineteenth-century harvest crisis and for many farmers the long delayed step of introducing reaping machines. Thereafter, at least till the early 1890s, mechanization and a contracting corn area provided farmers with the long awaited respite.[1]

The harvest labour market appears to have deteriorated faster in France and Germany than in Britain, notwithstanding the substantial post-1850 contraction of the British harvest labour force. For while the British harvest labour requirement reached its peak in the mid-1850s or perhaps even earlier, between 1850 and 1880 the French requirement grew by 20 per cent and the German by at least 40 per cent. Also relevant is that over this period both France and Germany were from time to time heavily engaged in manpower-consuming warfare; that their most active phase of railway building occurred between 1850 and 1870; and that, because their average size of farm was smaller than in Britain, the opportunities for harvest mechanization were correspondingly fewer. Average weekly agricultural wage rates in France increased by over 60 per cent between 1850 and 1882, and in some areas more than doubled. In Germany the 'dangerous overpopulation' and preoccupation with pauperism characteristic of the decades immediately after 1815 gave way from 1850 to complaints about emigration and general recognition of the improved condition of the working classes. On a large Rhenish estate annual wages of hands advanced by 100 to 120 per cent and those of labourers 45 per cent between 1853 and 1873. Harvest wages must have grown as fast if not faster.[2] In Prussia, farm wages increased by 125 per cent between 1849 and 1891-2, notwithstanding an expanding farm population.

Harvest labour scarcities were again assuming serious proportions in France by 1854, in which year was established the principle that soldiers could be set to work during crises. In the mid-sixties it was recommended that the government set up a central agency for the temporary mobilization of all available manpower during the summer months, especially at harvest, using the railways to distribute workers across the country. Sutherland observed in the late 1870s that 'the labour question is one of the most difficult with which French statesmen have to deal . . .

[1] J. Caird, *English Agriculture in 1850-51* (1852) pp. 517-18; *Farmers' Magazine*, Sept. 1853, pp. 200-6, Sept. 1859, p. 190, Oct. 1859, pp. 313-14, Aug. 1866, p. 170; O. Anderson, 'Early Experiences of Manpower Problems in an Industrial Society at War, Great Britain, 1854-56', *Political Science Quarterly*, LXXXII (1967) pp. 526-45.

[2] Kindleberger, op. cit., p. 233; Sée, op. cit., p. 332; W. H. Dawson, *The Evolution of Modern Germany* (1908) p. 271; W. Köllmann, 'The Population of Germany in the Age of Industrialization', in H. Möller (ed.), *Population Movements in Modern European History* (New York, 1964) pp. 101-2; J. Lapkès, *La Main d'Oevre en Allemagne* (Paris, 1926), p. 86.

throughout France generally one is met with loud complaints as to the scarcity, dearness and inferior quality of the labourer'. Harvest wages in some northern departments were at that stage as high and often higher than in most parts of Britain.[1]

Similar reports are available for most areas of western Europe.[2] In Hesse the universal complaint in the late 1860s was 'the great rise in wages and want of agricultural hands . . . one universal madness'. Migration, emigration and expanding agriculture caused Prussian farmers to look east for summer hands; after 1860 and in the 1870s there began their 'long drawn out wail' about rural depopulation, which despite mechanization and a heavy recruitment of foreign workers continued up to the First World War. Holland too experienced similar if less traumatic shortages after 1850, particularly during the Franco-Prussian War, as the old Hanoverian migrant flows began to dry up and young Dutch farm workers sought new fortunes across the border in the industrial Ruhr and Westphalia. Shortages were reported in Switzerland during the industrial expansion of 1870–80 and had become sufficiently acute by the 1890s to stimulate the formation of machinery syndicates in a number of cantons.

In eastern Europe harvest worker/corn area ratios deteriorated progressively after 1840. The Rumanian wheat area expanded by over 125 per cent between 1860 and 1900, the Russian by 70 per cent between 1870 and 1900, and the Hungarian over the same period by 75 per cent. It is hardly surprising that reaping machines were hard at work on some of the larger Hungarian farms in the later 1860s. On the Rumelian Plains migrant workers had become so expensive by 1884 that the government took the unprecedented and drastic step of introducing machines. Credit banks were set up in Serbia in 1893 for the purchase of agricultural machinery to insure against

---

[1] *JAP*, 21, pt. II (1857) p. 208; 30, pt. I (1866) pp. 120–1. Mr Sutherland's 'Report on the Agriculture of West Central France', in *R. C. Agriculture, Reports and the Assistant Commissioners*, I (1880) p. 813.

[2] R. B. D. Morier, 'Report on Land Tenure in the Grand Duchy of Hesse', in Probyn, op. cit., p. 436. The rural population of Hesse which had increased by 19 per cent between 1816 and 1834 and by 8 per cent between 1834 and 1861, declined between 1861 and 1864, ibid., p. 433. Clapham, op. cit., pp. 204–6. Dutch evidence was kindly provided by Dr Van der Poel of Wageningen. On Switzerland, see E. A. Pratt, *The Organization of Agriculture* (1904) p. 170. For Danish evidence, see H. Rainals, 'Report of the past and present state of the agriculture of the Danish Monarchy', *Journal of the Royal Agricultural Society*, XXI (1860) pp. 289–95; for Belgian evidence, see *R. C. Agriculture*, Reports of the Asst. Commissioners, I (1880) App. to Mr Jenkins's Report on Belgium, pp. 787–9; for Irish evidence see *R. C. Labour*, IV, pt. II (1893) pp. 5, 9.

'prejudiced crops due to the inadequate supply of labour'. Carniola had its 'unsolved farm servant problem' in 1893, while in Croatia efforts were made to disband the *zudruga*, the extended family farm unit, which it was claimed was chiefly responsible for manpower shortages and high wages.[1]

III

It is obvious then that to meet the increased crop demands and to offset reductions in the size of harvest workforces which we have noted there must have occurred over the nineteenth century a very substantial improvement in western European standards of harvest labour productivity. But equally obvious is that mechanization played but a very small part in this process. Efficient reaping machines became available in Europe only after 1850, and as Table III demonstrates their subsequent progress was slow and unimpressive.

Predictably the reaping machine gained ground faster in Britain than elsewhere in Europe because of the higher average size of farm and earlier decline of the harvest workforce. Even so, less than 30 per cent of the British harvest was mechanized in 1871, and it can be argued that the apparently rapid uptake of machines in the early seventies was in many cases a panic response to the rise of agricultural trades unionism. In the 1880s there were still many large farms in southern and midland England where hand-tool methods were exclusively employed. In Berkshire and Oxfordshire, at least, the scythe and heavy hook are still relatively fresh in the minds of the older generation of farm workers. In France the reaping machine was a great deal slower to take command. In 1856 the bulk of farm machinery elaborated by Jourdier in his *Le Materiel Agricole* consisted either of exhibition models of foreign origin, or machines confined to the farms of wealthy operators and 'taste leaders'. In 1892 the position was only slightly better. Clapham observed how even by this late stage the typical products of the application of nineteenth-century metallurgy and engineering to agriculture had not yet conquered even the largest French holdings. There is little basis for Kindleberger's contention that between 1850 and 1880 an 'enormous'

[1] *Annuaire Statistique*, 58 (1951) pp. 386–7; (for European corn production data) *JAP*, 32, pt. II (1868) pp. 266–7; D. Warriner (ed.), *Contrasts in Emerging Societies* (1965) pp. 248, 305, 329, 341–3, 361; Pratt, op. cit., p. 211. The Hungarian labour situation is closely detailed by S. M. Eddie, 'The Changing Pattern of Landownership in Hungary, 1867–1914', *Economic History Review*, 2nd ser., XX (1967) pp. 306–9 and especially 307n.

number of French rural workers had been freed by the reaping machine, unless of course we are prepared to accept manpower savings of less than 100,000 or less than 2 per cent of the adult workforce as an impressive level of defection from agriculture. In view of the high average farm size east and north of the Elbe the German performance was if anything less impressive than the French, but even though numbers of reaping

TABLE III

Harvest Mechanization in Western Europe: 1861–92[1]

		Nos. of reaping machines	Corn area mechanized* (millions of acres)	% of corn area mechanized
1880	Belgium	1500	0·09	4·1
1862	France	18000	1·08	3·4
1882	France	35000	2·10	6·8
1892	France	62000	3·72	11·5
1882	Germany	20000	1·20	3·6
1895	Germany	35000	2·10	6·0
1861	Gt. Britain	10000	0·60	6·8
1871	Gt. Britain	40000	2·40	27·7
1874	Gt. Britain	80000	4·80	56·4
1882	Holland	239	0·01	1·1

* = at 60 acres per machine.

machines grew dramatically after 1895 it was none the less significant that as late as 1907 only one-third of German farms from $5\frac{1}{2}$ to $12\frac{1}{2}$ acres, and two-thirds of those from $12\frac{1}{2}$ to 25 acres, owned machinery of any

[1] Sources: F. Dovring, 'The Transformation of European Agriculture', in H. J. Habakkuk and M. Postan (eds.), *The Cambridge Economic History of Europe*, VI (Cambridge, 1965), Table 58, p. 644; Dutch data supplied by Dr Van der Poel of Wageningen; areal data from Toutain (1961), op. cit., pp. 105–7, and European agricultural statistics detailed in *Agricultural Returns of Great Britain*, *passim*. Numbers of reaping machines in Britain (1861–71) are from contemporary estimates cited by P. A. David, 'Mechanization in Nineteenth Century Agriculture – Britain and America', unpublished paper read at The Centre for the Advanced Study of Italian Society Seminar, University of Reading, 20 Feb. 1968. The 1874 datum is an estimate from *Farmers' Magazine*, Aug. 1874.

kind. In the Netherlands stationary barn machinery was not yet general by the 1930s, with high levels of field mechanization mostly confined to a few farms in Zeeland and Groningen.[1] For much of southern and eastern Europe, mechanization, and harvest mechanization in particular, has been a post-Second World War phenomenon.

IV

How then, without machines, were the labour and labour-cost savings effected? The first and most obvious shift was to utilize more fully the local labour pool. In the labour-flush years of the post-Napoleonic War decades farmers were usually able to buy the services of local tradesmen, workers in domestic industry, and the wives and children of employees at relatively low cost. We can assume as well that during this period the degree of effort was often dampened, first because where wages were low and work scarce the labourer had little incentive to speed up the job, and second, because where family labour was well supplied, the small-farm family often preferred a more leisurely rate of work to a faster pace and subsequent inactivity. At times of high crop demand advanced wages or equivalent incentives could spur both to faster work tempos and longer hours. Employers discovered too that workers responded better to task work than to time work. From the 1830s the harvest became more and more a piecework operation under which terms it was not unusual for work to continue through the evening and, if the moon was full, often well into the night.[2] There was the further possibility that the cutting period could be extended by a few days if this did not involve too great a risk of heavy grain loss by shedding or spoilage. During the period 1815–34 farmers in eastern and southern England were often sufficiently rich in hands to secure the harvest inside a fortnight. One Hampshire farmer freely admitted that after ten days he was able to dismiss every hand, while on an East Anglian farm 300 men were once set reaping in a single day and a large crop of wheat was cut down in four or five days.[3] Other means at the farmers' disposal included

[1] Clapham, op. cit., pp. 170–1; Kindleberger, op. cit., p. 212; P. Lamartine Yates, *Food Production in Western Europe* (1940) pp. 118, 425–6.

[2] E. H. Hunt, 'Labour Productivity in English Agriculture, 1850–1914', *Economic History Review*, 2nd ser., XX (1967) pp. 280–92, argues convincingly the case that higher wages increased the supply of effort. After 1850 British agriculturists became more aware of the diseconomies of cheap labour. Thaër had discovered this before 1810.

[3] N. Gash, 'Rural Unemployment, 1815–34', *Economic History Review*, IV (1935) p. 187.

earlier cutting at the yellow-ripe stage of maturity to add perhaps a week to the front end of the harvest, and staggered sowing to phase out the ripening process.

In many of the more important cereal-growing areas, local supplies of labour were insufficient, even during the eighteenth century, to meet harvest demands and these areas therefore were heavily dependent on imported migrant workers. Indeed, these constituted for western Europe the most important and most widely exploited source of new supplies of harvest labour during the nineteenth century. This represented not only a satisfactory means of ironing out regional inequalities in the seasonal distribution of manpower but also it provided a solution to the problem of seasonal unemployment in peripheral upland, pastoral, and vine growing areas. Many flows were already well established before 1815. Thereafter as the populations of the source areas increased the volume of the flows grew considerably, their movements became more sensitive to regional shifts in demand, and their circulations became more international.

The numbers of Irish harvesters in England and southern Scotland increased quickly after 1815 to reach their peak in the late 1840s. By the 1820s it was already clear that in areas where cereal and fodder crop cultivations were expanding rapidly or where industry was having adverse effects on local farm labour markets, the Irish were wholly indispensable. Exploiting the different harvest timings of upland and lowland, north and south, clay land and light land, the Irish took two or even three harvests a season – moving between the Fens and the Wolds, the Cotswolds and the Vales, and the Tweed and the Carse in orderly succession. In the later 1840s they were probably responsible for 8–10 per cent of the British harvest and this was additional to the already very considerable contribution of the internal migrant flows.

Elsewhere in western Europe migrant flows remained largely internal to each nation until after 1850. In France the old circulations – the *Gavots* from Hautes and Basses Alpes, the *boquaux* from Terres Froides, Cremieu and Chambaran, the vineyard workers from Champagne-Mouton and the small proprietors from Yonne – all increased in volume over the post-Napoleonic War decades. By the late eighteenth century the Meaux region was already reported to be receiving 20,000–24,000 'strangers' a season. By 1840 the total number of migrant harvesters in France must have exceeded 250,000. Around 1850, the Belgian *sapeurs* (already well known in Loire, Beauce and Brie) extended their itineraries

77

to include the plateaux of Valois and Soissonnais while the 1850s saw also the first appearance of Bretons in the Paris region.[1]

The drying-up of many of the traditional migrant flows after 1850 and the lack of further sources of migrant labour supplies may partly explain why in Britain and France the reaping machine took on faster than in Germany. In Britain the Irish supplies declined sharply after 1850, and by 1880 were probably less than half what they had been in the years immediately after the Famine, while French access to external supplies was limited to relatively small intakes of Italians and Swiss in the south-east, Spaniards in the south-west and Belgians in the north-east. Germany on the other hand, and Prussia in particular, were able to tap the vast and extremely cheap manpower reserves of 'child rich' eastern Europe, when after the 1860s the internal migrant flows slowed down and the Swiss and the Dutch flows were unable to make good the deficit. In Prussia, Poles, White Russians and Austro-Hungarians fulfilled the same functions as hoers of roots and harvesters of corn as had the Irish in Britain during the second quarter of the nineteenth century. Their numbers increased significantly after 1900 as in the source areas supplies of new corn land began to run out and the first real symptoms of rural over-population began to develop. By 1910 the numbers of foreign seasonal workers in Germany exceeded 300,000 to which must be added at least an equal number of all-year-round migrant workers.[2]

This massive seasonal movement of manpower between pasture and arable, vine and corn, highland and lowland, and east and west, this drawing in of the peripheral areas into the mainstream of the developing economies, was perhaps the most outstanding feature of the western European farm labour market during the nineteenth century. The role of labour migration as a factor in agricultural development has been much neglected by economic historians, with the conspicuous exception of Redford whose observations of the Balkan flows during the Great War prompted his classic study of labour migration in Britain.[3] In eastern and Mediterranean Europe harvest migrations were if anything more spectacular than in western Europe. The plains of Thrace and Rumelia, like those of Hungary, coastal Italy and southern Spain, were gigantic

[1] Tresse, loc. cit., p. 355; Chatelain, loc. cit., pp. 494–9 passim; D. Faucher, Le Paysan et la Machine (Paris, 1950) p. 75. See also Sée, op. cit., App. p. 104; P. Vigier, La Seconde République dans la Région Alpine, II (Paris, 1963) p. 68.
[2] Clapham, op. cit., pp. 204–9; F. Wunderlich, Farm Labour in Germany (Princeton, 1964) pp. 23–4. In 1913 numbers exceeded 435,000: Lapkès, op. cit., p. 45.
[3] A. Redford, Labour Migration in England, 1800–1850 (Manchester, 1926).

LABOUR SUPPLY AND DEMAND IN AGRICULTURE

summer labour sponges. Seasonal migration was for a long time an integral feature of the corn-growing economies of the American West. Some migrations were recognizably inter-continental. The Poles who trekked 1,000 miles from the Vistula to the Seine, and the Mexicans who spread themselves as far as the Great Lakes were out-distanced by the *golondrinas*, the Piedmont peasants who left Italy for the flax and wheat fields of Cordoba and Santa Fé (Mexico) in November, harvested corn in southern Cordoba and Buenos Aires (Argentina) between December and April and returned to Italy for the spring-planting in May. As one historian observed about long-distance seasonal migration in the nineteenth century: 'It is possible that if such movements were to be gathered together they would reveal an amazing frequency of proletariat globe-trotting, a frequency unequalled by the upper-class traveller of the richer countries.'[1] At any rate they helped satisfy at relatively low cost the labour requirements of western European and New World agricultures during the critical proto-industrial phase of economic growth.

V

Technological change, when it appeared, first took the form not of mechanization but of a switch from lower into higher working capacity hand tools. Thus, as an intermediate step, the heavy hook, or more often the scythe, superseded the traditional toothed sickle and smooth reap hook as the standard corn harvesting tools, first for the spring grains, barley and oats and then for the bread grains, wheat and rye. The various competing tools and methods are illustrated on pages 80–1. The heavy hook took two forms: the straightforward large-size reap hook (*la grande faucille, le volant*) as found in north-west France, but probably obtaining too in many other areas of Europe, and the altogether larger and more specialized 'bagging hook' and 'stick' which was extensively employed in southern Britain. The scythe took four forms: the S-handled scythe with heavy hard-steel blade common to Britain and North America; the straight 'poled' scythe (*la faux Picarde, der Sense*) with a hammered mild-steel blade, general over most of continental Europe except

[1] R. F. Foerster, *The Italian Emigration of our Times* (1919) p. 37, cited in F. Thistlethwaite, 'Migration from Europe overseas in the nineteenth and twentieth centuries', in Möller, op. cit., p. 78; ibid., p. 77. For Eastern European migrations see Warriner, op. cit., pp. 16, 247–8, 260–6, 273. For U.S.A. migrants see L. F. Cox, 'The American Wage Earner', *Agricultural History*, 22 (April 1948) pp. 95–114 *passim*. For Italian internal migrations, see Foerster, op. cit., pp. 36–7, 60, 532–3.

79

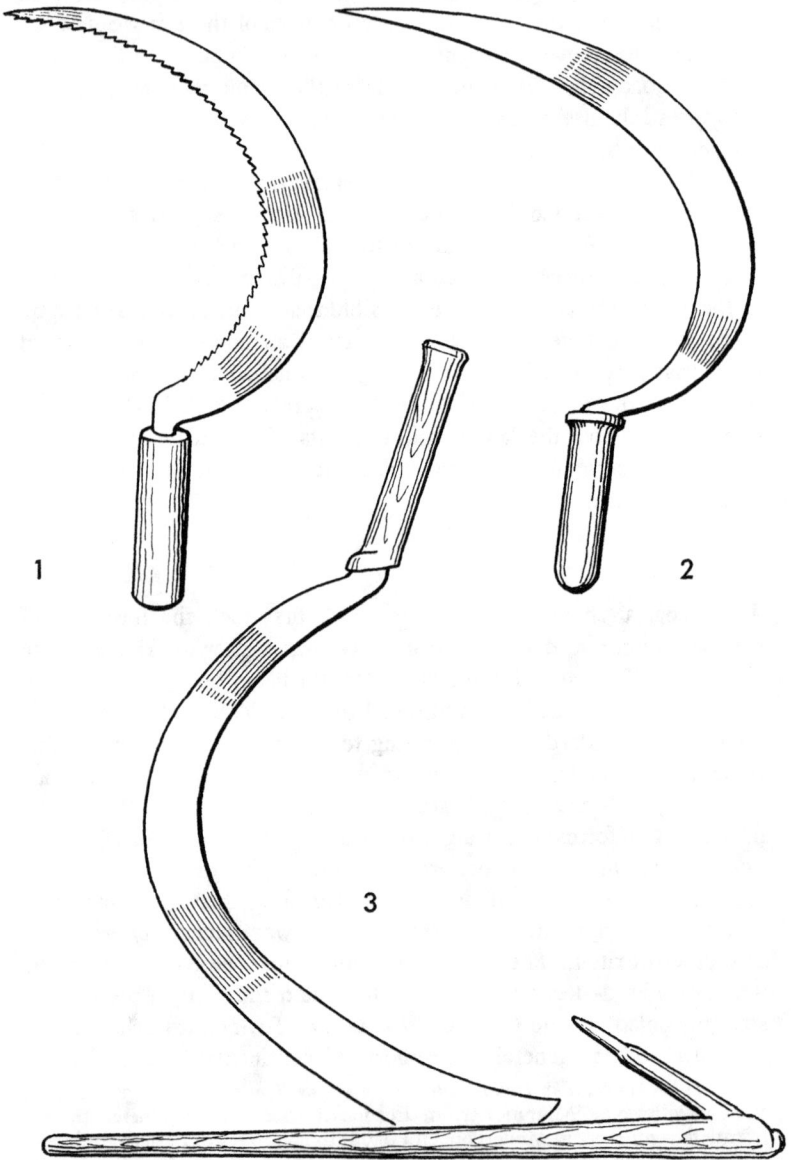

1. German serrated sickle. (British sickles generally carried a narrower blade than Continental models.) 2. Scottish smooth-edged reap hook. 3. English bagging hook and stick.

Scandinavia; the short-handled, one-handed scythe (*la sape, das Sichet*) and its hooked stick (*la pique, das Sichethasen, das Haken*) used in the Low Countries, North France and north-west Germany; and the Y-shaped, two-handled scythe developed in north-east Scotland about 1830 as a

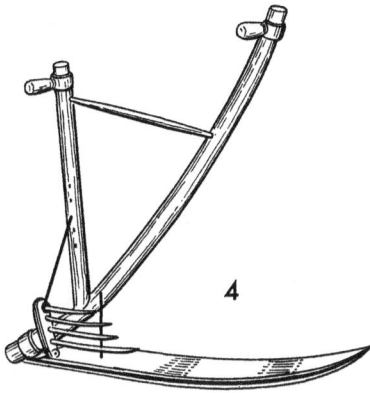

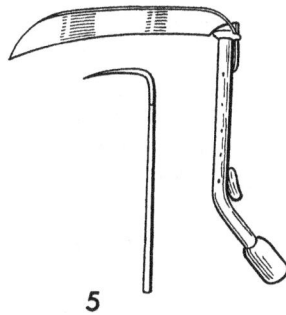

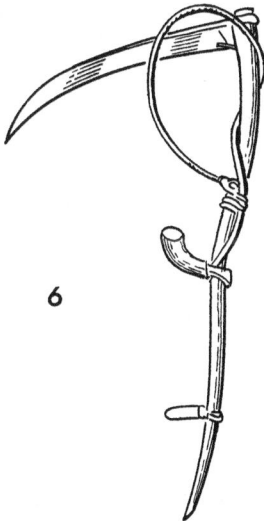

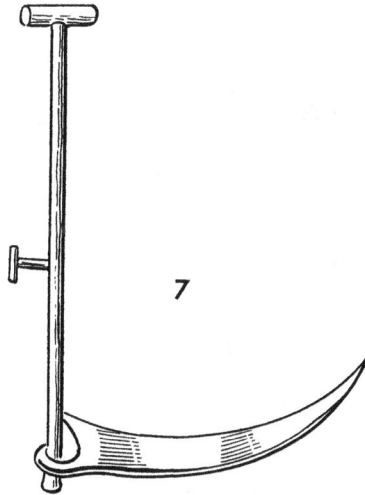

4. Y-shaped Aberdeen Scythe with 'cradle' attachment. 5. Flemish short-handled *sape* and *pik*. 6. English S-shaped scythe with cast-steel blade and 'cradle' attachment. 7. European poled scythe with hammered mild-steel blade.

specialist grain harvesting tool, and confined to Scotland, the extreme north of England and parts of Northern Ireland. The adaptation of the scythe from a grass into a corn harvesting tool owed a great deal to the cradle (*le crochet* or *râteau, das Gestell*), a wooden fork-like construction, or the bow (*le playon, das Bügel*), a construction of looped sticks or bent wire, which were attached to the heel of the blade and helped the mower to lay the corn down regularly to give an even swathe.[1]

The labour-saving advantages of the heavier tools are immediately obvious, but because of their high linkage-labour requirements relative to the hand reaping tools these were much less spectacular than crude cutting rates suggest. In Britain the notional labour savings of the heavy stroking and slashing tools relative to the small reaping tools were approximately as follows:

Work Rates and Labour Requirements for Competing Harvest Methods in Britain

A = Cutting rate per worker-day (in acres)
B = Ratio linkage workers to cutters
C = Worker days per acre

	Wheat			Barley and Oats		
	A	B	C	A	B	C
High reaping (sickle)*	0·35	1:7	3·6	—	—	—
Low reaping (sickle)	0·25	1:5	4·8	0·33	1:5	4·0
Low reaping (reap hook)	0·33	1:5	4·0	0·4	1:5	3·3
Bagging	1·0	2:1	3·0	1·3	2:1	2·2
Mowing (binding and sheaving)	1·1	2:1	2·7	2·0	2:1	1·5
Mowing (leaving loose in swathe)	—	—	—	2·0	5:1	0·75

* Excludes autumn clearance of stubble.

Thus in the primary field operations the labour-saving potential of the bagging hook and scythe relative to the hand reaping tools was of the order 25–35 per cent and 35–45 per cent in the harvesting of wheat, and 33–45 per cent and 55–65 per cent in the harvesting of barley and oats.

[1] The various tools and methods are discussed in H. Stephens, *Book of the Farm*, III (1844) pp. 1048–1105; G. H. Schnee, *Encyklopädie der Landwirth-schaft*, I (Brunswick, 1860) pp. 637–47; F. Kirchhof, *Der Deutsche Landwirth* (Leipzig, 1847) pp. 144–50; *Maison Rustique du XIX siècle*, I (Paris, 1839) p. 296·

Making certain assumptions about labour requirements in the linkage operations of binding and stooking to compensate for lower yields we can show similar labour savings over the range of French tools, with the labour savings of the *sape* relative to the scythe and sickle being approximately the same as those of the English bagging hook. For Germany Thaër's data suggest the labour savings of the scythe relative to the sickle at upwards of 25–30 per cent.[1] Other advantages stemmed from their cut closer to the ground which increased the supplies of feeding and bedding straw, while the quicker harvest allowed an earlier start on autumn ploughing and an earlier resumption of root and sugar-beet cultivations.

The close correlation between the adoption of faster tools and diminishing harvest labour supply is readily established.[2] Resistance to new methods was always strongest where labour was most abundant and where the incentives to labour-saving innovation were consequently lowest. The real issue was essentially that of economic incentive versus technical constraint.[3] Adherents to the sickle complained that the heavy tools were wasteful of grain, that compared with the gentle meticulousness of hand reaping theirs was a brutal assault which resulted in excessive spillage and shattering of ears. It was objected too that mowing or slashing was less efficient than hand reaping on twisted and badly laid crops, that they made for high grain loss and left an untidy and difficult swathe. This constraint was perhaps most operative on rich nitrogenous soils such as those of the East Anglian Fens and the Dutch and Belgian polderlands, which partly explains the failure of the scythe to take command there until relatively late on in the nineteenth century. The applicability of the scythe to uneven, highly ridged or rock-strewn terrains was also doubted and extensive rolling and stone clearance were deemed essential prerequisites for its introduction. It was demonstrably true that the sickle with its regular sheaves, even stubbles and shaven ricks provided a standard of technical excellence which the heavier tools were unable to match. Economically it was argued that sheaves of mown or slashed corn increased costs in the secondary operations of carting,

[1] *Maison Rustique*, I, op. cit., p. 297; *JAP*, pt. I (1837) p. 557; 33 (1869) p. 874; Schnee, op. cit., I, p. 95; Thaër, op. cit., I, p. 103.

[2] Collins, loc. cit.

[3] For discussions of technical advantages and disadvantages of competing methods see sources detailed on page 82, note 7. I do not agree with the modern interpretation by Professor A. Steensberg, *Ancient Harvesting Implements* (Copenhagen, 1943) pp. 232–47, which stresses the topographical and physical influences on the dissemination of the scythe in western and northern Europe and under-emphasizes the economic factors.

stacking and threshing. The bread corns, wheat and rye resisted the innovations longest. This was not altogether surprising in societies not long removed from the threat of famine, but it reflected too the much higher straw resistance of wheat which rendered the mowing of a battered crop a long and arduous business. As late as the 1860s it was still being argued in Scotland that the scythe could never be transformed into a successful wheat harvesting tool. This was especially true as long as farmers insisted upon cutting at the dead ripe stage of maturity when the risks of grain losses were greatest. Significantly the spread of the heavier tools was closely correlated with the uptake of the cradle and the adoption of the practice of cutting grain at an earlier stage of maturity.

That in the longer run the scythe and heavy hook overcame most physical constraints reinforces the view that the main determining factors of change were economic rather than technical. The chronology of innovation was in any case not dependent on environmental conditions. Scythes were faster to gain ground on the rugged fields of North Sweden than in the southern lowlands, faster on the rich alluviums of East Essex and the clays of the Vale of York than on the light soils of the southern Cotswolds and the Wiltshire Downs, and faster on the Massif Central than on the plains of Arles. Today over much of southern Europe and the Middle East the scythe is predominantly a mountain tool while in Spain it has always been confined to the highlands of Cantabria and Galicia.[1] Similarly, the practice of bagging originated in the heavy land districts of the London Basin, the Devon Hams and the Herefordshire plain, while in France *la grande faucille* appeared first on the small rocky farms of Brittany. Perhaps the skill factor was more important than the topographical. It was generally agreed that the scythe required strength and long practice for efficient operation. Gasperin described mowers as the aristocrats of the rural workforce.[2] Wherever farmers were dependent for their harvest on female or part-time industrial workers then the adoption of the scythe and heavy hook was predictably slow. Again, where farmers relied heavily on migrant harvesters whose hand-tool preferences were much more resistant to pressure of demand than those of resident workers, the possibilities of rapid change were less. It was largely the objections raised by sickle-wielding migrants from the Yonne which persuaded Brie farmers to abandon their experiments with the scythe during the First Empire, while in the English midlands the strict adherence of the

[1] *Private Communication*, Spanish Agricultural Attaché (London, Jan. 1969).
[2] Cited Vigier, op. cit., I, p. 28n.

Irish to the sickle was reckoned the chief constraint on the introduction of the scythe there in the 1860s.[1] Conversely, though, migrants were sometimes important diffusion agents of new methods. It was the Bretons who introduced the heavy hook into the Paris Basin, the Belgians who gave the *sape* to northern France, the West Surrey men who brought the bagging hook on to the South Downs and the Aberdeen mowers who carried the scythe into the Scottish Lowlands. Significantly, by the later nineteenth century, both the Irish and the Yonne migrants had abandoned the sickle and equipped themselves with scythes or heavy hooks.

VI

Up to the mid-eighteenth century the sickle and reap hook were the predominant corn harvesting tools in Europe. The scythe was confined to south Britain, the Low Countries, the Rhineland and a few areas of Denmark, France and Switzerland. Nowhere, except in Flanders and Hainault, had the practice of mowing been much extended to the bread grains, wheat and rye.[2] Yet by 1900 the scythe or the heavy hook had become the chief and in most places the exclusive hand harvesting tools through western Europe and were soon to become so in eastern Europe and the Balkans. Only in Portugal, Italy and Spain was reaping with small tools still the common mode.

Over this broad international front the chronology of change was inevitably complex. But for western and central Europe at least we may distinguish several reasonably distinct phases of innovation approximately corresponding to the longer run fluctuations in the harvest labour market already described. Thus the second half of the eighteenth century may be viewed as the experimental and 'early adoption' phase of the revolution. The Napoleonic Wars saw an accelerated uptake of faster working tools and through the farming literature a much wider awareness of their labour and labour-cost saving possibilities. The two or three decades after Waterloo were for most areas a period of hiatus in which innovation slowed down and in which the small reaping tools were able to regain some lost ground. It could even be argued, in view

---

[1] Chatelain, loc. cit., p. 498; H. Evershed, 'Farming of Warwickshire', *Journal of the Royal Agricultural Society*, XVII (1856) p. 480.

[2] *Museum Rusticum*, II (1764 edn) pp. 33–5; F. Benoit, *Histoire de l'outillage rural et artisinal* (Paris, 1947) p. 45; P. Lindemans, *Geschiedenis van de Landbouw in België*, II (Antwerp, 1952) pp. 58–65; Steensberg, op. cit., pp. 232–47; D. du Monceau, *The Elements of Agriculture*, trans. P. Miller, I (1764) pp. 331–3.

G

of the post-war shifts away from spring corns into wheat, that in France and Britain the sickle may have controlled an even larger area in 1835 than in 1815. The years 1835–80 and particularly 1850–80 constituted the 'majority adoption' phase of the hand-tool revolution, in which the small tools were almost everywhere superseded and their use confined to a few areas such as western Ireland and the Alpine regions where farms were small and corn values low. Throughout continental Europe, and up to the mid-1860s even in Britain, the scythe and the heavy hook gained ground much faster than the reaping machine between 1850 and 1880. The usual progression was for the scythe to be extended first from grass to barley and oats and then further extended (along with heavy hook) to the bread grains, wheat and rye.

Some time in the first half of the eighteenth century the East Riding of Yorkshire became the first area in Britain to apply the scythe regularly to wheat, while in Devon, Hereford and the inner Home Counties the practice of 'bagging' or 'slashing' wheat evolved either out of smooth hook reaping or as an extension of a method already applied to pulses. In France the *sape* penetrated from Flanders and by the 1760s the conventional Picarde scythe, probably with a cradle attachment, was being applied to barley and oats in parts of Beauce, Brie and the Gatinois, in which last area according to de Monceau rye and even wheat were mown by farmers bordering the Forest of Orléans. Considerable interest in the scythe was aroused in France and even in England by the widely publicized experiments of M. de Lille who in the 1750s brought in Flemish workmen to demonstrate the tool and to instruct local workmen in its use. By the Revolution the mowing of spring corn was already well established in some of the specialist corn-growing areas of the north and the Paris Basin. Early nineteenth-century Danish references to the 'Brunswig' or 'Braband' sickle suggest that by 1800 the *sape* had already penetrated North Holland and had overflowed on to the North Germain Plain, presumably having been borrowed and subsequently rediffused by the Brunswick and Hanoverian migrant workers. We can only assume that during the second half of the eighteenth century, as in France, the practice of mowing spring corn had spread outwards from its earlier concentrations along the Rhine.[1]

In Denmark, Upper Sweden and North Finland, eighteenth-century progress was spectacular by most other European standards due, it would appear, to combined pressures of short seasons and extensions of the cultivated area on already scarce supplies of harvest labour. In

[1] Du Monceau, op. cit., pp. 331–51; Steensberg, op. cit., p. 239.

Denmark, where the mowing of barley was reported in 1640, the cradle scythe gained ground quickly after 1735 so that by 1820 this and the 'Brunswig' sickle were dominant everywhere except on the North Sea Islands and in parts of West Jutland. In Upper Sweden and Swedish-speaking districts of Finland the later eighteenth-century spread of the scythe may have been as rapid. Progress here was a great deal more impressive than in Norway, where in 1750 mowing was practised only within a narrow radius of Oslo and where the victory of the scythe was almost wholly a nineteenth-century phenomenon.[1]

The 1790s ushered in twenty years or so of accelerated and in some areas extremely vigorous innovating activity. In Britain progress appeared rather more impressive than in France and Germany. The practice of bagging wheat diffused outwards from its earlier strongholds to conquer West Dorset, and much of the Home and Welsh Marcher counties, as well as a few areas of Wales where 'much corn and too few hands' had brought about its importation from Herefordshire and Shropshire. The mowing of wheat became standard practice in East Dorset and East Kent as well as in parts of the East Midlands where the method had spread in from the Yorkshire Wolds. The scythe also advanced northwards and westwards from the East Riding into the North Riding and Teesside and into the Vale of York. In Scotland the scythe established itself in the north-east and was experimented with here and there in the Lothians and central Lowland counties. But perhaps most indicative of the anxiety to speed up the harvest were the highly organized if abortive attempts to popularize the Flemish *sape* in both Hampshire and Ireland. In France activity was much more regionalized, being mostly confined to the northern corn-growing departments. Following the traumatic labour shortages of 1794–6 the Commission d'Agriculture et des Artes gave its official blessing to the scythe while an efficient government-sponsored national scythe-making industry was set up to improve the quality and quantity of the domestic product and to lessen the country's dependence on Austrian and German sources of supply. During the First Empire the *sape* established itself in north-eastern France, Mont Blanc adopted the *grande faucille*, the Narbonne region embraced the cradle scythe, while in L'Ain the scythe was introduced into the spectrum of harvest hand tools for use in years of high crop demand.[2] In Germany, too, the scythe came into more extensive use during this period as farmers recognized more and more the need for faster tools to avert crop losses on shedding overripe corn.

[1] Steensberg, op. cit., pp. 232–42.   [2] Tresse, loc. cit., pp. 354–8.

Attempts were also made 'to invent instruments for the purpose of perfoming the various [linkage] operations appertaining to the getting in of the corn'.[1]

This relatively high level of activity did not long survive the peace. In a few areas such as north France, east midland counties of England, and north-east Scotland, the scythe and heavy hook did manage, however, to consolidate their wartime gains. But elsewhere the flow of innovation was temporarily halted and the sickle was often able to recover lost ground as in some areas the scythe was abandoned or else reserved only for exceptional seasons.[2] In parts of southern England the sickle was sometimes able to displace the time-honoured scythe in the harvesting of heavy crops of barley and oats. Inertia was most apparent in areas such as Lancashire, the Scottish Lowlands and in the Paris Basin which attracted large and increasing numbers of cheap sickle-wielding migrant harvesters, or in areas such as the midland clay vales where opportunities for land reclamation, heavier cereal cropping and extended root and fodder cropping which would have created a greater and competing demand for summer labour were extremely limited.

Retrospective testimony from all three major western European countries leaves little doubt that the hand-tool revolution did not regain its momentum until after 1835. In south Germany the sickle was still the customary tool for wheat, and in some locations even for oats, in the 1840s. Before 1835 the scythe was still very much a minority tool in Scotland and northern England, and virtually unknown in Ireland, while in England probably as much as 70–75 per cent of the wheat area was harvested by the sickle or reap hook. The official *Enquête* of 1848 leaves little doubt that the sickle was at this stage still the predominant harvest tool over most of France. In the light of this and other evidence it is impossible to give much weight to Tresse's view that the French hand-tool revolution was more or less complete by 1845.[3]

The case for a turning-point in the mid-1830s is well evidenced for Britain. In 1837 it was reported how the sickle was 'formerly the only implement for the reaping of wheat. . . . Of late years it [the scythe] has come very much into use and seems to be gaining ground for cutting down every kind of grain.' By the 1840s the farming press was rich with reports of rapid change, of 'a new aera' in harvesting technology and

---

[1] Thaër, op. cit., pp. 381–2.   [2] Chatelain, loc. cit., pp. 498–9.
[3] Kirchhof, op. cit., pp. 146–7; W. Hamm, *Die Grundzüge der Landwirthschaft*, I (Brunswick, 1850) pp. 641, 660–1, 644; Chatelain, loc. cit., pp. 496–7; Tresse, loc. cit., pp. 354–8.

'very considerable advances . . . within the last few years in many parts of the Kingdom towards the adoption of a more judicious and economical mode'.[1] In 1870 the bagging hook had become the chief wheat harvesting tool over southern, central and west midland England, the scythe had conquered most of eastern England, Scotland north of the Forth and the best part of Wales and had strongly established itself in southern and eastern England, while the sickle was soon to disappear from the East Anglian Fens, the midland clays, Cheshire and the English and Scottish border counties. In some areas, notably in Ireland where serious harvest labour scarcities did not occur until the 1890s, change was to continue through and beyond the 1870s. When the reaping machine eventually took over from hand tools this was seldom achieved without the prior insertion of some form of intermediate hand-tool technology. Even in southern Scotland where hand reaping often gave way directly to machines this was not before the toothed sickle had been superseded by the (25–33 per cent) faster smooth reap hook.

The spread of the scythe and heavy hook in France is especially well documented by the official *Enquêtes* of 1848, 1852 and 1866. Chatelain is probably right in his belief that the scythe did not really become popular until after 1850, but there is strong evidence nevertheless that important gains had been secured during the previous fifteen years. Successful introductions of Flemish and Picarde scythes were being reported in 1839. In 1847 it was noted how 'dans ces dernières années' the scythe had been introduced. The first *sapes* came on to the plateaux of Valois and Soissonnais in 1845, while already by 1850 the scythe was beginning to replace migrant sickles in the important wheat growing districts of Brie and Beauce.[2] Evidence for an uptake in the mid-1830s is provided by the official scythe production and importation statistics for 1831–46, detailed in Table IV on page 90.

The numbers of scythes available more than doubled between 1831–3 and 1844–6 while numbers of home-produced scythes grew from 77,000 in 1816-17 to 287,000 in 1831, and to almost one million in 1844–6. The technological improvements in French metallurgy made during the first half of the nineteenth century enabled French scythe makers to compete effectively with the Austrian and German craftsmen. The appearance on the home market of a high quality native product may have helped break down farmers' traditional hostility to the scythe, just as in Britain

---

[1] *Farmers' Magazine*, Aug. 1845, p. 96; *British Husbandry*, II (1837) p. 189.
[2] Chatelain, loc. cit., pp. 496, 498; *JAP*, II (1838-9) pt. II, pp. 44-5.

improvements in the design and construction of scythes and bagging hooks during the 1830s may have had the similar effect of broadening workers' hand-tool preferences. Yet it would be incorrect to overstate here the importance of this supply factor, for there is little evidence that the uptake of faster tools was at all closely correlated with ease of access to their source of supply. Just as the proximity of Sheffield did not tempt West Riding farmers to adopt the wheat scythe on any scale until the

TABLE IV

Totals of Imported and Home-produced Scythes in France, 1831–46[1]
(in millions)
1831–33 = 100

1831	0·589	99	1837	1·168	196	1843	1·131	190
1832	0·609	102	1838	0·778	131	1844	1·213	204
1833	0·589	99	1839	0·770	129	1845	1·133	190
1834	1·410	237	1840	1·076	181	1846	1·317	221
1835	0·849	143	1841	0·872	146			
1836	0·943	158	1842	0·855	144			

1830s, so around Toulouse, the chief scythe-manufacturing centre of France, the corn scythe did not come in until the 1840s. Significantly, in Styria, historically the oldest and most renowned scythe-making region of Europe, corn mowing was still in the experimental stage in 1836.[2] We must conclude then that demand rather than supply was the chief determining factor in the growth of the French scythe industry after 1830, while the stability of the French grass area between 1831 and 1846 must suggest that the bulk of new scythes were used in the corn harvest. If we assume that of the 625,000 extra scythes in use in 1844-6 compared with 1831-5 90 per cent were applied to corn, and that each harvested an average of ten acres a season, then we can calculate that between 1831 and 1846 the scythe was extended to a further 5·6 million corn acres, or rather more than 15 per cent of the total French corn area.

Between the *Enquêtes* of 1848 and 1866 the scythe, *sape* and *grande faucille* had conquered a vast area of France. By 1870 the *grande faucille* was established in Ardeche, in Auvergne, the Plains of Arles and over large areas of the north-west; the *sape* over most of northern France from L'Oise to the Belgian frontier, and the scythe most elsewhere. But,

[1] *JAP*, 3rd ser., V (1852), pt. II, pp. 32–5.
[2] Chatelain, loc. cit., p. 496; Blum, op. cit., pp. 190–1.

as in Britain, there were a number of areas where change was then still incomplete, especially on the Alpine regions of the south-east where the transition from sickle to scythe was still continuing in the early years of the present century.[1]

The German evidence suggests that the period 1850–80 was one of similarly rapid change, particularly in the south and east which had been relatively unaffected by the earlier waves of innovation which had transformed harvest technology in the north and west. In the 1850s the scythe had reached eastern parts of Baden while a decade later in Würtemburg the sickle survived only on small farms. The eastern spread of the scythe into Prussia is more problematical. Even so, by 1860 the use of the sickle was reported more or less confined to mountain areas and small highly fragmented farms.[2] Further into Europe, in Czechoslovakia, the sickle was the chief tool in the 1830s, although here and there on a few estates in Bohemia, Moravia and in the adjacent regions of Carinthia, Silesia and Upper and Lower Austria the scythe had already found favour. In western Czechoslovakia it had become the dominant tool by the 1850s, although complete victory was delayed until at least the 1880s. In the mountain districts of Austria the sickle managed to hold out until the Second World War.[3] Between 1850 and 1930 the scythe extended its empire to Russia and the Balkans. In 1907 Russian scythesmen were being employed as seasonal workers on East Prussian estates, which fact would perhaps have surprised Peter the Great who, in the early eighteenth century, had abandoned in disgust his attempts to familiarize the peasantry in the use of this 'good and needful' tool.[4] Later evidence from Galicia and Poland suggests that the sickle still prevailed as the women's tool in the 1930s,[5] although by this stage most male workers were using the scythe. By the 1930s too the scythe predominated in Greece and much of the Balkans, while in parts of Bulgaria (where around Sofia the sickle was still general in 1930) teams of men could

[1] *JAP*, 33 (1869) p. 874; Chatelain, loc. cit., pp. 497–9; *Arts et Traditions Populaires*, XI (1963) p. 289.

[2] Benaerts, op. cit., pp. 146–7, *Reports on Tenure of Land in Europe, 1869*, I (1870) p. 83; Schnee, op. cit., I (1860 edn) p. 639; W. Löbe, *Handbuch der rationellen Landwirthschaft* (Leipzig, 1855) p. 282.

[3] Blum, op. cit., pp. 163–4, 191; F. Kutnar, 'Zur Problematik der Saat und Erntetechnik in der Zeit des Bach'schen Absolutismus', *Scientific Studies of the Czeckoslovak Agricultural Museum*, 7 (1967) pp. 83–107; E. Burgstalker, 'Die Sichel als Getreideschnittgerät in Oberösterreich', *Zeitschrift für Agrargeschichte und Agrarsoziologie*, 11 (1963) pp. 63–77.

[4] Dawson, op. cit., p. 290; B. H. Sumner, *Peter the Great and the Emergence of Russia* (New York edn, 1962) pp. 143–4.

[5] Steensberg, op. cit., p. 243.

often be seen scything gigantic fields by hand in the early 1960s, despite an extensive use of combine harvesters on the Dobruja Plains.[1] The appearance of the scythe in Turkey is a relatively recent phenomenon, it having been introduced into the country from Greece. In Israel scythes were introduced by German settlers in the 1890s, but while they have never really caught on in the Middle East as a whole there are strong indications that the *qahuf*, the Arab equivalent of the large sickle, is gaining ground there.[2] Further west in the Mediterranean the scythe has failed to establish itself in Spain except in the mountain provinces of Cantabria and Galicia. In Italy, though, the practice of mowing corn came into the Lombardy plain during the Napoleonic Wars and was general on many large estates in the 1890s. In the Mezzogiorno the scythe was adopted in a few areas in the late 1930s and 1940s and now enjoys a certain status on hill and mountain farms where mechanization is impracticable.[3]

Nor was the usefulness of the scythe wholly confined to European agriculture. Rogin, in his classic study of farm tools and implements in the U.S.A., describes how owing to 'the scarcity of labour and the relatively extensive methods of farming pursued' the cradle scythe progressively displaced the sickle from the end of the Colonial period, to become general in most large grain-farming areas in the eastern states by 1800 and subsequently to be taken by settlers across the Alleghennies on to the Great Plains.[4] But although the reaping machine appeared in the mid-west in the 1840s, on the small farms of New England the 'cradle' continued to displace the sickle after 1850. Further north in Canada, the cradle scythe (*le javelier*) was general in Montreal by the early 1840s, but did not gain the upper hand in Quebec province until after 1845, and during the period 1845–65 enjoyed considerable popularity until eventually it was superseded by the machine.[5]

[1] G. Servakis and C. Pertountzi, 'The Agricultural Policy of Greece', in O. S. Morgan (ed.), *Agricultural Systems of Middle Europe* (New York, 1933) p. 155. Yet there were only 606 reaping machines in Greece in 1929, ibid., p. 152; G. Mountfort, *Portrait of a River* (1962) pp. 41, 49; I. T. Sandars, *Balkan Village* (Lexington, 1949) p. 45.

[2] S. Avitsur, *Implements for harvesting . . . [in] . . . Eretz Israel* (Tel Aviv, 1966) pp. i–xxvii. Cutting rates with the *qahuf* are up to four or five times higher than those of the standard *qalush* or *dunam* sickles.

[3] Field observations by the author and Dott. P. Raffone of the Cassa per il Mezzogiorno, June 1968.

[4] Leo Rogin, *The Introduction of Farm Machinery . . . [in] the United States* (Berkeley, 1931) pp. 69–72, 125–32.

[5] R. L. Seguin, 'L'usage du Javelier en l'État du Québec, Canada', *Arts et Traditions Populaires*, XI (1963) pp. 282–9.

VII

This paper has tried to demonstrate the extent to which expanding agricultures in industrializing economies were afflicted by seasonal shortages of labour and how in the harvest operation these were offset, initially at least, by the more efficient use of society's total manpower resources, and by the adoption of cheap non-mechanical labour-saving technologies. Western European proto-industrial agriculture made some exceptional demands on both its manpower and its technology. Economically it was important first that improvements in farm output were secured through low capital-consuming technologies and, second, that agricultural production should not be adversely affected by contractions in farm labour supply such as invariably occurred during upswings of the trade cycle, during wartime, or in seasons of high crop demand when labour supply and demand schedules converged. Socially, however, it was important that the technology was sufficiently labour-consuming to absorb a farm population whose numbers continued to increase up to and in most cases beyond 1850, and which usually did not decline until relatively late on in the nineteenth century. In short, the technology mix had to provide enough discontinuity to guarantee sufficiently high levels of work output during the peak activity periods when labour shortages were most likely to develop, but at the same time to provide enough continuity to obviate serious unemployment over what for the majority of farm workers constituted the key earnings period. Thus during the critical harvest operation the required improvements in output per worker were secured both along and by shifts of the technical spectrum, that is by effort expansion and the more intensive use of migrant labour, and by the uptake of an inexpensive intermediate labour-saving technology of improved hand-tool methods.

The relatively late appearance of the reaping machine in western Europe and its subsequent slow uptake cannot, as Dovring has already argued,[1] be explained away by any technological failure on the part of the agricultural engineering industry. It is inconceivable that British engineers, who by 1850 had already perfected that highly complex item of farm machinery, the steam thresher, could not, if the demand had existed, have achieved comparable standards of technical excellence in the development of the reaping machine.[2] Nor, for some decades after

---

[1] Dovring, loc. cit., p. 646.
[2] Threshing machines were altogether quicker to catch on than reaping machines. In 1882, for example, France and Germany possessed between them

1850, were reaping machines able to provide European farmers with a realistic solution to the harvest problem. First, because farm layout and terrain often prevented the efficient use of field machinery; second and more importantly, because at prevailing wage levels, only the largest farms could provide a sufficiently high seasonal work-load to justify its adoption, for unlike the threshing machine the reaping machine was not really a 'divisible input'; and third, because in many areas farmers were socially constrained from introducing a technology which might create unemployment among the resident workforce. The scythe and heavy hook had the advantages of neutral scale and low cost; they provided sufficient gains in work output for farmers, up to and for some time after 1850, to be able to resist the more spectacular factor savings offered by the machine.

In nineteenth-century Europe improved harvest labour productivity was the end result therefore of a complex social and economic process of which technology was but one component. The efficiency of a technology must be measured not so much by its discontinuities as by the extent to which it satisfied the factor proportions of its environment.

ACKNOWLEDGEMENTS

The author would like to thank the Keeper of the Museum of English Rural Life, University of Reading, for providing material for illustrations. Plates 1, 3 and 4 are taken from H. Stephens, *Book of the Farm* (1844) III; Plate 2 is from the Museum of English Rural Life's photograph collections (original held by Hereford City Library); and Fig. 6 is taken from T. Hennell, *Change in the Farm* (Cambridge University Press, 1934), p. 103.

585,000 threshers but only 55,000 reapers, ibid., p. 644. The apparent anomaly that farmers were prepared to mechanize a winter operation but not a summer one is a problem all by itself. However, we can recognize: (*a*) the cost divisibility of the threshing machine through hiring; (*b*) that threshing had no intermediate technology; (*c*) that the flail was an extremely labour-intensive tool requiring the services of strong adult males, thus preventing any extensive use of casual and 'inferior' labour, such as was abundantly available for the harvest.

4 Agricultural improvement in Japan 1870–1900

R. P. DORE

[The editors and publishers wish to thank the University of Chicago Press for permission to reproduce this article, first published in *Economic Development and Cultural Change*, Vol. IX, 1, part 2, 1960.]

Not the least remarkable feature of Japan's economic development in the nineteenth century is the way in which the growth of industry was matched by an increase in the productive capacity of agriculture. If industrial investment was largely financed out of the surplus produced by agriculture, this was not, at least, a process of mere spoliation. Agriculture was not entirely starved of capital, nor did the policy emphasis on industrial development mean that the task of increasing the productivity of agriculture was neglected. The purpose of this paper is to examine some of the mechanisms by which this improvement was achieved; the way in which new methods, tools and crop strains were evolved and diffused; the agents of, and the motives for, research and experiment; the channels of communication and the incentives for application. Following the general theme of these papers one concern will be to assess how far the improvement was self-generated within agriculture, and how far the stimulus came from the urban centres of commerce, industry and governmental authority.

Continuities

The phrase 'the greatest innovation is the idea of innovation itself' is a striking and in many ways a true one. It points up the contrast between

NOTES

In the footnotes to this article the major sources have been abbreviated as follows:
MZKJS: Nōrinshō, Nōmukyoku, (*Meiji Zenki*) *Kannō Jiseki Shūroku*, 2 vols. (1939).
NT: Nōrinshō, *Nōmu Temmatsu*, 6 vols. (1952–7).
NNHS: Nogyo Hattatsu Shi Chosa Kai, *Nihon Nōgyō Hattatsu Shi*, 10 vols. (1953–8).

95

a tradition-bound society in which antiquity is the greatest guarantor of both techniques and values, and, on the other hand, a society receptive to change, confident of the possibility of self-betterment and instinctively tending to identify novelty with progress. Japan's *bummei-kaika* period, the early Meiji 'Enlightenment' with all its innovating enthusiasms, seems a typical case of sudden transition from the one to the other. In the realm of techniques, however, the picture of pre-Restoration Japan as a tradition-bound society requires qualification. As T. C. Smith has recently shown,[1] there was considerable innovation in agriculture – slow cumulative changes, evolved and actively preached by men who deliberately recorded and experimented in the conscious hope of making useful innovations. It was, moreover, a literate and articulate concern. Of the large number of works on agriculture written, and often printed, in the late Tokugawa period many, of course, were simply distillations of traditional lore copied from earlier works, many were simply exhortations to frugality and diligence; a large proportion were hints on edible fungi and herbs for use in famines. But a number were concerned with ways and means of improving production, by switching to new varieties and new crops, by adopting tools and fertilizers and methods discovered in other parts of the country, by introducing new subsidiary employments, and sometimes by applying the lessons of the writers' own experience and conscious experimentation.

This, then, is something to be borne in mind when considering developments after 1870. There was already a tradition of gradual improvement. There was a class of literate farmers, and some samurai, who were intelligently aware of the desirability and the possibility of change. The Meiji Restoration greatly intensified and diffused that awareness by opening up new sources of technical knowledge and by making the innovator one of the heroes of the new society. But some continuity there was nevertheless. One of the best illustrations, perhaps, is the publication in 1880, with a preface by the Minister of the Interior, of a proposal for land reclamation in Chiba written by Sato Shin'en in 1833.[2]

There was continuity in another sense. Tokugawa improvements in agricultural productivity had been actively promoted by the fief governments. Land reclamation schemes, in particular, had almost always been at the initiative of the fief. It was therefore natural that the new central government of the Meiji period should take a positive role in agricultural improvement.

[1] *The Agrarian Origins of Modern Japan* (Stanford, 1959).
[2] *Naiyō Kei-iki*, see *Nihon Sangyō Shiryō Taikei*, I (1926) p. 1010.

The Central Government

It is with the role of the central government that our inquiry can best begin. Almost as soon as the Meiji Government was established, a section concerned with agriculture was created in the Ministry of the Interior. This, after several changes in location and organization, variously amalgamating with and separating from the section concerned with commerce and industry, eventually emerged, in 1881, as the agricultural half of the new Ministry of Agriculture and Commerce.[1] The main emphasis of the activities of this department varied with changing circumstances. In the first decade one predominant concern was, of course, fiscal. It is no accident that for a short period in 1872 and 1873 the Department was a sub-section of the Taxation Bureau of the Ministry of Finance.[2] Later, with the firm establishment of the land tax system and its reduction to a matter of routine, this preoccupation disappeared.

A second major concern in the first decade was land reclamation. The title of the Department when first established in February 1869 was the 'Reclamation Bureau'. Land reclamation in this period had, of course, a dual purpose – to find some work for the now displaced samurai, and to 'increase the wealth of the country'. Of these two aims the former was the most pressing. It was the starting-point of Okubo's arguments when, as Minister of the Interior shortly before his death, he proposed to the Dajokan a grandiose scheme which would settle some 13,000 samurai families on new land at the cost of six million yen.[3] The *shizoku-jusan* scheme did do much on these lines, though not, with a total expenditure for all, including industrial, enterprises of only three million yen,[4] quite on the scale Okubo envisaged.

A third concern was with the promotion of exports and the reduction of imports by the substitution of home-grown products. The table of contents of the first half-dozen farmers' bulletins published in 1874–6 show this early concern with foreign trade in the frequency of articles on silk production, on the reception of Japanese tea in foreign markets, and reports on successes in home-growing foreign cotton.[5]

Fourthly, the major continuing concern was with the general improvement of production wherever and however this could be done – with

[1] A good summary of these administrative shifts is to be found in MZKJS, I, pp. 5–10.
[2] Ibid., p. 6.   [3] Ibid., pp. 24–5.
[4] Kyōto Daigaku Kokushi Kenkyushitsu: *Nihonshi Jiten* (1955).
[5] Ibid., p. 204.

making two blades of grass grow where only one grew before. 'Agriculture is the base of the country; if agriculture flourishes then the country prospers; if agriculture declines then the country is on the road to ruin.' So spoke Shinagawa as head of the Agricultural Promotion Bureau at the first agricultural congress in 1881,[1] and we may note in passing an important implication of his words. In thus enunciating one of the tenets of modern developmental economics, Shinagawa was, in fact, merely reiterating the views of orthodox Confucian conservatives of the Tokugawa period. For the Confucianist it was a fine and noble thing to sweat in the muddy bosom of nature (if not quite as fine and noble as fighting), whereas industry and commerce were ignoble occupations. One cannot overlook the importance of this tradition in ensuring that the Meiji government did not make the mistake of throwing agriculture overboard in a passionate pursuit of industrial modernity. (Later, of course, the tradition turned sour and in a defensively virulent form played a large part in the reactionary Japanism of the thirties.)

The Department pursued its goals by a variety of methods. The first decade was largely devoted to the assimilation of the new possibilities opened up by contact with the West, particularly after the emissaries returned from the Vienna Exposition of 1873 laden with plants and seeds and farm tools. The Shinjuku experimental station, established in 1872, was largely devoted to testing them. In 1876, for instance, it was growing 313 strains of foreign wheats and only 247 Japanese (though only Japanese rice). There were 398 foreign trees and grasses compared with 76 indigenous varieties.[2] By this time, too, the experimental station had got permission to use the remainder of its foreign tool purchasing budget to start its own factory and make farm tools on foreign models.[3] Already they had moved from the stage of adoption to the stage of domestication. (This factory remained a government enterprise longer than most and was not sold off until 1888.[4])

All this time Japanese officials and students were being sent abroad to study foreign agriculture, and foreigners were being hired as advisers in Japan. A total of twenty-two foreigners were employed by the Department before 1880 (including five Chinese experts in silk and egg incubation) and another dozen by the Kaitakushi which was concerned with the development of Hokkaido – the experimental grounds *par excellence* for foreign agriculture.[5]

[1] *Nōdankai Nisshi* in NNHS, 1, p. 671.
[2] MZKJS, 1, p. 125.　　　　　　　　　[3] MZKJS, 1, p. 26.
[4] Nakayama Taishō (ed.), *Shimbun Shūsei Meiji Hennen Shi*, 7 (1940) p. 14.
[5] MZKJS, 1, pp. 541–4; 2, p. 1804.

Inevitably, this initial enthusiasm for things western did not last indefinitely. The useful new crops were quickly assimilated; the new methods often proved unsuitable. After 1880 the emphasis turned back somewhat to more traditional concerns – improvement within the framework of Japanese agriculture, by developing new strains of traditional crops, and by diffusing more widely the best practices of particular regions. Shinagawa, in the speech quoted above at the agricultural congress in 1881, went on to talk of the danger 'in leaping ahead to the new of neglecting what is good in the old', a danger just as great as conservative resistance to innovation. It is significant that the congress itself was a congress of 'old farmers' – the heirs of the Tokugawa tradition of intelligent experimenting farmers – and they were called together expressly for the purpose of exchanging information about traditional practices in their regions.

More germane to the present discussion are the methods used to diffuse the knowledge thus accumulated. First, there was the exhibition method. Agriculture played an important part in the Promotion of Industries Exhibitions, five of which were held between 1877 and 1903.[1] In addition a number of national prize shows for various particular products were held, especially after 1880, and from 1874 to 1885 a permanent Museum of Agriculture was maintained in Tokyo.[2] The experimental stations themselves were also designed as permanent exhibitions. One concern of the government when it secured the Shinjuku site was that it should be in a well-frequented district.[3]

Secondly, the Department was charged with the promotion of agricultural schools and colleges. Directly under its own control was the Komaba college which later became the Faculty of Agriculture of Tokyo University. In addition the Kaitakushi had its own famous agricultural college at Sapporo, the home of the ambitious Mr Clark. By 1883 the Komaba school had three departments – of agriculture proper, of chemistry, and of veterinary medicine. It then had a staff of 13, 4 of them foreigners, and 107 students, 46 of them supported by official scholarships.[4] A survey of their graduates in 1886 showed that almost without exception they had taken jobs with local prefectural governments.

Thirdly, the Department was charged with direct promotional and extension activity. Some of the relevant functions listed in the Department's charter of organization as drafted in 1874 were:[5]

[1] MZKJS, I, p. 463.   [2] MZKJS, I, p. 517.   [3] MZKJS, I, p. 517.
[4] MZKJS, I, p. 269.   [5] MZKJS, I, p. 22.

1. To keep an eye open for all inventions and improvements which the Minister might reward with prizes and honours.

2. To make plans for the loaning of seeds and implements, or of cash to purchase them, to individuals and organizations.

3. To investigate all suggested schemes which could contribute to the national welfare, to test experimentally the principles involved, to make detailed estimates of costs and benefits and make suitable recommendations to the Minister.

The procedures followed were enterprising and *ad hoc*, most important in providing official encouragement for local initiative. In 1876, for instance, a farmer in Nara Prefecture forwarded to the Department a detailed record of experiments with rice strains which he had been carrying out since 1863, together with some samples of particularly successful varieties. Within a week a congratulatory letter had been written and he had been sent a number of fruit trees and asked to try them out. His own varieties were tried out in the Shinjuku testing grounds.[1]

The Department early set about the task of formalizing and expanding its channels of communication. In 1874 it began publication of a bulletin and in 1877 prefectures were instructed to appoint regular correspondents who should report anything likely to be of value to the Department and receive the Department's Bulletin, as well as specific answers to specific queries, in exchange. At first it was envisaged that these should be prefectural officials, but from 1880 private individuals were appointed and allowed to correspond directly with the Department (by unstamped letter).[2] By 1885 there were nearly 2,000 farmers receiving the Department's bulletins.[3]

The next step was the organization of local agricultural associations. Again these were the result of a mixture of local and central government initiative. It was in 1880 that the Department issued a circular to all prefectures urging the establishment of agricultural improvement associations. This was not an original idea; a number of Seed Exchange Societies and Agricultural Discussion Societies had already been formed, in some cases entirely on private initiative, in some cases with the assistance and encouragement of prefectural governments.[4] But again the Department played an important broker's role in diffusing and lending authority to the idea. The response in the prefectures seems to have

[1] NT, I, pp. 11–12.   [2] MZKJS, I, p. 297.
[3] MZKJS, I, p. 285.   [4] NNHS, I, pp. 653–5.

been rapid, and the growth of local associations was further accelerated by the congress of 'old farmers' (three from each prefecture) when it was held in Tokyo the following year. These became the founder members of the Japan Agricultural Association which developed out of the congress. At the same time they were key figures in the local associations. Thus began the organization which eventually grew into the Imperial Agricultural Association. By 1899, the year in which an Agricultural Associations Law gave legal backing, some government funds and model constitutions to the local associations and bound them into a tight pyramidical structure, the correspondent system could be abolished as superfluous. In 1905 membership in the associations became compulsory for all farmers.[1] And eventually a solid and well-staffed organization emerged which was able to take over the semi-official functions of statistical reporting and, during the wartime period of total mobilization, of rationing, crop requisitioning and planting controls as well.

It is difficult to assess the total effect of the central government's activity. The Department's staff was not large – a total of ninety ranking officials in 1877 and perhaps fewer ten years later.[2] Nor was it particularly well endowed with funds: in 1890 the total budget for the Ministry of Agriculture and Commerce was less than a million yen, a thirtieth of that of the Ministry of Finance, and less than a third of the allotment for the Imperial Household. Of that sum at least five-eighths was devoted to the administration of the national forests.[3]

It seems certain, though, that this small Department played an essential organizing role which greatly magnified the effect of local individual initiatives. In its early formative and improvising years, too, it seems to have shown a bold and apparently infectious reformist drive. But, in the very nature of things this enthusiasm could not last for ever. Routinization set in, and with it complacency. Yanagita Kunio, reflecting on his official life in 1909 has some very pertinent things to say.[4] One great difference he perceives between his childhood days and the present is that people are less interested in argument and discussion.

> The fact that officials rarely issue memoranda and suggestions [for improvement] may be because the volume of business they have to deal with has increased, or because the boundaries of each person's authority have been fixed and no one likes to take the risk of treading on another's territory. Anyhow, the fact is they have ceased.

[1] NNHS, 5, p. 330.   [2] MZKJS, 2, pp. 1811–20.
[3] Okura-sho, *Meiji Zaisei Shi*, 3, p. 549.
[4] *Jidai to Nōmin* (1910) repr. in *Yanagita Kunio Sensei Chosaku Shū*, 4, p. 5.

The changing role of the government is matched by a change in the people. 'It seems a long time, too, since patriotic citizens, heedless of their own poverty, would journey long distances to the capital to present petitions and policy memorials. The establishment of the Diet was the turning-point.' Now people only present petitions in their own interest. The patriotic league has become the pressure group; the farmer anxious to report an idea which might contribute to the national welfare has given place to the applicant for a subsidy.

Prefectural Governments

The work of prefectural administrations in the development of agriculture in early Meiji was similar to that of the central government and at least as important. In many respects they played an intermediate role, working in obedience to the instructions of the central government, running tests of new varieties and reporting back to the Shinjuku experimental station and its successors, redistributing tools, livestock and subsidies sent them from the central Department. But prefectural governments also took their own initiatives, subsidizing their own private schemes, importing their own seeds and making their own tests. At the 1881 congress of 'old farmers' a number reported initiatives in livestock breeding which had been carried out by their prefectures. We have already seen that a few Agricultural Improvement Societies were already established before the central government sent out their instructions, some of them supported by prefectural or county funds. In the matter of education, too, by 1880 at least seven prefectures had independently established agricultural colleges – often combined with an experimental station – financed out of local funds.[1] Later the Ministry of Education took an active part in the matter of agricultural education, and its outline regulations for agricultural schools, promulgated in 1883, provided a further stimulus to local initiative. By 1886 the total number of provincial schools had grown to sixteen, including a number run by counties or groups of villages.[2] Ten years later the number was forty-six, about half being prefectural schools and half operated by lower government echelons.[3] Nine of the latter specialized exclusively in sericulture, and in 1886, at least, the average size seems to have been only about forty pupils. Nevertheless this was an important beginning.

It is not always easy to trace the source of initiative in these matters, but it is certain that a good deal depended on the energy of prefectural

[1] MZKJS, 2, p. 1585.   [2] MZKJS, 2, pp. 1588–92.   [3] NNHS, 3, pp. 590–4.

officials, even in the matter of implementing the suggestions and recommendations of the central government. In 1884, for instance, the central government issued model regulations for producers' unions,[1] the aim of which was to secure regular grading and quality controls over marketed rice. Not all prefectures took active steps to form such unions; some did nothing; some merely passed the model regulations on to village offices and left it at that.[2] Others actively urged and supervised the formation of such unions and some, such as Chiba, considerably amplified their sphere of competence and made them responsible for supervision of the whole process of rice cultivation and laid down specific rules to be followed from seed selection to the baling of threshed rice.[3]

The prefectural officials were, moreover, closer to the ground. They were in direct contact, if not with the mass of farmers, at least with the upper strata of village leaders. There was a difference between the central government mailing a circular recommending the selection of seed by salt water or the drying of sheaves on wooden racks, and the prefectural office issuing the same recommendations to village officials. In the latter face-to-face relationship with its still strong *kanson-mimpi* – 'the official is noble, the people base' – overtones, a recommendation was likely to be taken as an order.

In some cases, indeed, the order was made explicit. Miyagi Prefecture, for instance, issued in 1878 compulsory regulations concerning the threshing and grading of rice, and penalties were prescribed for infringement.[4] This offended against the liberal philosophy which Matsukata brought into economic policy, and in 1881 the Ministry ordered the regulation to be withdrawn. Things were different twenty years later, however. Beginning in 1896 with Miyazaki, a number of prefectures issued by-laws (*kenrei*) enforcing practices which were considered beneficial to rice cultivation. Between 1896 and 1904, for instance, at least twenty-four prefectures ordered that rice seedbeds should be oblong in shape and not more than four feet wide (to facilitate weeding and the control of pests – especially the rice borer – from the sides) and eight of these included penal provisions, ranging, in some cases, up to ten days' imprisonment or a ten-yen fine.[5] Other prefectures forbade the use of lime fertilizer (and were somewhat discountenanced when a few years later the Ministry announced that experiments had disproved the current old wives' tales about the dreadful effects of using lime).[6] Others ordered the regular spacing of rice plants in rows to facilitate weeding

[1] NNHS, 3, pp. 332–4. [2] NNHS, 5, p. 48. [3] NNHS, 3, pp. 336–7.
[4] NNHS, 5, p. 20. [5] NNHS, 2, p. 131. [6] NNHS, 4, p. 743.

and a number tried to impose rice grading regulations by fiat.[1] The inclusion of penal provisions became more common during the Russo-Japanese War, but many were abandoned not long thereafter. The 'extension by the sabre method' as Japanese historians call it in honour of Frederick the Great was not altogether popular. Clashes between police or agricultural officials and the farmers were frequent. In one district the spaced planting method was reputedly known as the wine-bottle method after a famous occasion on which an inspector, having fortified himself on a *shō* of *sake*, charged into a field brandishing the bottle over his head and began to uproot irregularly planted rice. He was promptly set upon and beaten for his pains.[2] However, such epic incidents go recorded while the doubtless far more common incidence of compliant submission has to be inferred from the fact that the improvements recommended did in fact become standard practice.

The Village

In a country the size of Japan it would seem unlikely on the face of it that the sort of governmental efforts we have been describing could have had much overall effect. A few prefectural by-laws, a few million yen's worth of tools and seeds distributed, the training of a few hundred graduates of agricultural colleges, the organization of a couple of thousand agricultural correspondents, would not seem to have much chance of leavening the conservatism of some five million farming households. And, if the nation's farmers had been individual, and individualist, entrepreneurs, the effect might indeed have been small. But they were not. The fact that farmers lived in small, tightly packed hamlets, the fact that these hamlets displayed a great degree of community solidarity backed by numerous forms of co-operative activity and until recently by the collective legal responsibility for tax payments, and the fact that these communities were for the most part traditionally inclined to accept paternalistic, authoritarian leadership – all these had the effect of greatly magnifying the results achieved. The 'old farmers' who gathered for the 1881 congress were working farmers of the traditional leadership stratum, men as conscious of their moral duty to guide their fellow villagers into better ways, and as confident of their right to do so, as they were devoted to good farming as an end in itself. Hear one of them, from Hyogo prefecture, reporting to the congress:[3]

[1] NNHS, 4, pp. 751–94.   [2] NNHS, 4, p. 108.
[3] NNHS, 1, p. 683.

The poor quality of rice in recent years is due in part to the ending of the old fief quality inspections and in part because people cut early and thresh roughly in order to get on with planting winter wheat. To counteract this, about twenty-two or three villages got together, and we decided on a 'stay-the-sickle' rule. People are not allowed to cut their rice until the reddish tinge appears. Farmers who are very hard up [and need money or food badly] can appeal to the village authorities and a section of their fields will be marked off which they are allowed to cut.

Another from Aichi says, during the discussion on rice bales:[1]

I hear that there is a village in Mikawa where they have established a farmers' union which has got out a detailed list of rules for the yearly round of farm work that the farmers must abide by. One of these is that you must always use last year's [tougher] straw for the rice bales.

In this way a few energetic 'old farmers' with traditionally supported authority could alter the farming practices of whole villages. The new rules were in an old tradition. It was no fresh and intolerable invasion of the farmer's independence that he could not cut his rice when he wanted to. He was used to village rules which prescribed the precise number of cups of *sake* which each guest could drink at his wedding, or which made it a community, rather than an individual, decision whether he could convert upland to paddy. This tradition greatly magnified the efficacy of the new Agricultural Associations which developed after 1880. They provided a new organizational framework in which the old pressures for conformity could be mobilized explicitly for the control of cultivating methods. At the second 'old farmers' congress in 1890 a Kyoto farmer reported:[2]

We set up an inspection committee [in the Agricultural Association] whose job it was to tour the village [covering each farmer] three times in the process of ploughing and planting. Reports were written and when the harvest came we took sample cuts, and then awarded prizes on the basis of a combination of the earlier reports and the quality of the harvest. This is one way of encouraging lazy farmers to work. Count Shinagawa [former head of the Agricultural Department of the Ministry] praised this highly. His phrase was: 'the landlord's footprints turn to dung', by which he meant, of course, that their walking

[1] NNHS, I, p. 699.　　　[2] NNHS, I, p. 657.

round the owner-farmers' and tenants' land, and remonstrating with the indolent was worth a good dose of fertilizer.

The organization of prize shows – *himpyōkai* and *kyōshinkai* – became, in fact, one of the prime functions of the village Agricultural Associations in the decade or two following 1890. One strong impelling motive was to improve the quality, and so raise the price, of rice, particularly – since the associations' leaders were generally landlords – of the rice paid to landlords in rent. But they soon, as in the example quoted, extended their concern to the whole productive process. A Niigata document outlining the prize system spells out in detail the method of judging, with prizes awarded for eight separate stages of cultivation, and – characteristically revealing the paternalistic tone of the whole affair – for the farmer's 'general behaviour' as well.[1]

A charming caricature of the beehive nature of the Meiji village, though one written with serious prescriptive intent, is the novel, *The Model Village (Mohan-chōson)*, published in 1907 by that fiery scholar and founding father of the modern *Nōhon-shugi* school of anti-urban back-to-nature thinkers, Yokoi Jikei.[2] The model nature of the village derives entirely from the energetic leadership of the dedicated mayor. As the visitor questions villagers concerning the recent innovations the constant preface to the replies is: 'Yes, the mayor has paid particular attention to that problem.' 'Thanks to Chairman Mao and the Communist Party,' one echoes, and indeed the village is like nothing more than a Chinese commune. There is a village hospital run by graduated taxation, there is a citizens' hall with a crèche where the children play with model agricultural implements, and a communal restaurant which provides everyday meals in busy seasons and no-host party meals to eliminate competitive entertaining. The visitor is puzzled not to be offered tea at the houses he visits until he realizes that this is one of the rules of rationalized living, designed to eliminate useless conspicuous hospitality.

There are many communal farming activities, co-operative glass-houses, co-operative livestock breeding, co-operative incubators for the chickens. Mostly, however, farming is still on a family basis, but with a great deal of communal direction overlaid. Holidays, for instance, are fixed for the whole village, and on every week-day bells ring out to mark the hours at which farmers should go to their fields, the hours at which

[1] Furushima Toshio and Morita Shirō, *Nihon Jinushi Sei Shi Ron* (1957) p. 289.

[2] Reprinted in *Yokoi Hakase Shū*, 5 (1924).

they may take a luncheon break, the hour to come home. And work and play are rigidly divided:

> disorderliness was the mayor's chief dislike and even at rice-planting he forbade singing while at work. At first people felt deprived and upset and there were many who jeered at the mayor's prejudices, but now they are extremely grateful for the great results. . . . The custom of girls dressing up at rice-planting and making it a time for choosing brides has automatically disappeared. One no longer sees the brash young men of the village teasing the girls while they are at work.[1]

By way of compensation there are billiards at the citizens' hall, a 'Morals Club' for the young men, dramatic clubs and choirs which sing pure, wholesome and improving songs to replace the deplorable bawdiness of traditional village ditties.

It is the Protestant ethic, all right; and yet Professor Yokoi's vision was not, after all, so far-fetched. At least one biographical account of a university graduate who returned to his native village, shows him working, with some success, on just these lines – with a temperance society and all.[2]

It is worth noting, however, that the mayor's influence in the model village, and the influence of the village leaders in the actual nineteenth-century village, was not necessarily a mere matter of naked authority. The 'old farmers' were able to secure their effect because the rules were not just their rules but 'village rules'. Their authority derived its legitimacy from the fact that in form, and to a varying degree in substance, the whole village gave its consent. Their rule was to guide the consensus rather than to issue orders. At the 1881 congress a Hyōgo man (and it is perhaps significant that it was a Hyōgo man and not someone from the mere authoritarian north) expressed his confidence that the matter of improving rice quality could soon be dealt with through the Agricultural Associations. In the associations which had just been formed in his prefecture[3] 'The officers were all elected from the farmers, and since the organization rests on a mutual contract (*meiyaku*) there is no doubt that its decisions will be rigidly observed.' Even when the authoritarianism of the landlord leaders was evident it was often made palatable to the villagers by the fact that the leaders were patently sincere in their efforts

---

[1] *Mohan Chōson* (*Yokoi Hakase Shū*, vol. 5) pp. 306–7.

[2] The autobiography of Sōma Kokkō as reported to me by Professor T. C. Smith. I have not been able to trace the details of this publication.

[3] NNHS, 1, p. 682.

to improve their fellows. It was part of the Confucian virtue of benevolence that they should be.

It is also worth noting that the growing commercialization of agriculture did not necessarily destroy the co-operative unity of the village. Unlike industrial entrepreneurs farmers were not in direct competition with each other – no single farmer's operations were big enough to affect the market. Hence there was no powerful economic incentive to keep the secret of successful improvements to oneself.[1]

Landlords

In a sense the influence of landlords has already been discussed. The 'old farmers', the village leaders who organized the Agricultural Associations were for the most part landlords. Particularly in so far as they used the constraint which could be exercised through the Association to improve the quality of rent rice and to forbid the use of lime fertilizer which was supposed to damage the fields, they were often as much concerned with raising the standards of their own tenants – to their own pecuniary profit – as they were with fulfilling a paternalistic duty towards their fellow-villagers, owner-farmers and the tenants of other landlords included. But this is not the sum total of the landlord's role; quite apart from their influence exerted through the village they also exercised a certain amount of direct control over the activities of their own tenants.

With few exceptions Japanese landlords were not, as in many sharecropping systems, joint entrepreneurs with the tenants, providing tools and seeds and sharing the proceeds. There was, however, considerable local variation in the extent to which the landlord-tenant relation was merely an impersonal contractual one or, on the other hand, was a personal relation in which protection and guidance were exchanged for service and submission over a whole range of life activities quite beyond the renting of land. The variation was reflected in the ease with which the fixed rental to be paid in kind could be adjusted for a poor harvest. When this was regularly done, even for moderate falls below average yields, not only was the landlord usually in a position to exercise a paternalistic authority over his tenants, he also had a strong economic incentive to exert that authority to improve his tenants' agricultural

[1] A point made, apropos of American agricultural innovations in the nineteenth century, by A. H. Cole, *Business Enterprise in its Social Setting* (Harvard, 1959) p. 112. I am grateful to Professor T. C. Smith for drawing my attention to this interesting passage.

competence. It is probable that in the early Meiji period the vast majority of landlords fell into this paternalistic category, and moreover the vast majority still farmed directly themselves.

It is not surprising, then, that many landlords exercised close direction over their tenants' cultivation. In 1888 the Ministry held a long correspondence with Shizuoka Prefecture concerning a certain farmer called Maruta who was reported to get a crop of six *koku* to the *tan*. Maruta provided a long detailed exposé of his methods, but it appeared that the crop in question had been raised by a tenant on Maruta's land, though presumably under Maruta's close supervision.[1] Perhaps few landlords exercised such direct control, but a good number acted to pass on prefectural authorities' suggestions about the shape of seedbeds, spaced planting and the like as 'orders' to their tenants. Some specified an interdiction on the use of lime in a written tenancy contract.[2] Others used the prize competition method. Furushima reports on a Niigata landlord who held prize competitions for his own tenants' rent rice for several years before they were replaced by village competitions organized by the Agricultural Association. Tenants who produced a superior product were rewarded with prizes of mattocks and sickles. At the subsequent feast, seating order was determined by standing in the competition, and it was a rule that those at the head of the list would be addressed by the landlord as *Mr* X (*dono*, at least) the rest without such polite suffixes.[3] Other landlords used more tangible incentives. An Osaka farmer reported at the old farmers' congress that in his village landlords reduced rent by as much as a tenth of a *koku* per *tan* if it was paid in rice of the best quality.[4]

Tenants were not always, at any rate, responsive to instructions *not* backed by economic incentives. In at least one case, the landlords borrowed police authority. The *Chōya Shimbun* reported in 1888 that sericulture was spreading rapidly in the San-in district, thanks to the initiative of the prefectural and county officials. In one county in Tottori officials had persuaded landlords to turn over as much as eight *chō* to mulberry. The landlords were agreed – provided their tenants did not object. The tenants were summoned to the county office, but they refused to go, complaining that they would starve – presumably in the interval before the mulberry began to produce. The county chief, accompanied by the police chief and secretaries, set out for the village. Police rounded up sixty or more tenants at the school and the county

[1] NT, I, pp. 19–30.
[2] NNHS, 2, p. 156.
[3] Furushima and Morita, op. cit., p. 248.
[4] NNHS, I, p. 686.

chief began his lecture. One woman fainted from excess of indignation, whereat a farmer seized a stick and began to lay about him. He was restrained, but, according to the newspaper account, 'amity was not restored'.[1]

The decline in landlord influence is quite clearly charted in the growing numbers of tenancy disputes from the time of the First World War. It was in part the result of a general loss of submissiveness on the part of the 'lower orders' of Japanese society. In the particular case of the landlords its effect was intensified by what Japanese historians refer to as their growing 'parasiticization'. As the period wore on, fewer and fewer actually cultivated land themselves. Fewer and fewer knew or cared enough about farming to advise or instruct their tenants.

The Entrepreneur

The Meiji period also saw the emergence of a new type of farmer – the capitalist entrepreneur. Typically he was an ex-samurai; he usually bought, or acquired as a gift, unreclaimed land; he usually started a new experimental type of Western farming; he usually had a government subsidy, and he usually did not last long. An example of a successful type of samurai entrepreneur was Karasawa Annin.[2] A samurai of Aizu, a fief scholar and official, he was imprisoned for anti-Imperialist activity at the time of the Restoration. Released, he set off, in 1873, to start a ranch in the northern tip of Honshu. He was given a government subsidy, employed two Englishmen for five years as advisors, and by 1876 was able to show the Emperor on a visit 180 head of cattle of mixed Western and indigenous breeds, and 24 horses. He also experimented with various new crops and carried out afforestation schemes. By 1889 he had created a village as an appendage to his ranch which he then left to his son. He himself moved to Tokyo to establish selling outlets for the ranch's products. He became founder of the Japan Livestock Association before he died a few years later.

Not all were as successful, by any means. Tsuda Sen, another ardent ex-samurai 'Westernizer' who had been to the Vienna Exposition in 1873, started a mulberry and dairy farm on some 180 *cho* of land in Chiba. After a few years, however, he admitted defeat and let the land out to tenants.[3]

---

[1] *Shimbun Shūsei Meiji Hennen Shi*, 7, p. 44.

[2] See *Dainihon Nōkō Den* (1891), reprinted in *Nihon Sangyō Shiryō Taikei*, 3, pp. 1025–7.

[3] Sakurai Takeo, *Nihon Nōhonshugi* (1935) p. 53.

Another successful case – a co-operative village in the hills above Tsuruoka founded by a group of retainers of the local fief – perhaps gives a clue as to why Tsuda failed. These ex-samurai, too, were enterprising innovators; they rapidly developed high-quality silk-worm egg production and the village still supplies the bulk of the demand from Yamagata Prefecture. But they started off on the traditional small-holding, family farm system.

In other words, the frequent failure of these innovators is probably ascribable to the same reason as prompted numbers of traditional large-scale farmers to cut down the size of their farms and let out land to tenants – the fact that the relative levels of rents and farm wages (somewhat raised by the opportunities for industrial employment) combined with the relative efficiency of hired and family farm labour, made tenancy a more profitable proposition. Even the ranches often developed into a tenancy system, with breeding cows leased out to tenants. In thus falling into the traditional pattern of agricultural organization, however, the new ex-samurai entrepreneurs sometimes brought a new style of energetic management into their tenancy operations. An example is the Mitsubishi enterprise in Niigata which, early in the 1890s, instituted a system of *compulsory* interest-free loans of fertilizer to their tenants.[1]

The entrepreneurial function was, perhaps, more important in another field – in the food processing and distribution industries. The silk factories, the sweet potato processing plants, the tea export companies, and the sugar-beet companies undoubtedly had a major effect in stimulating switches to more profitable crops. Very often these, too, had government subsidies. One of the major fights in the first Diet revolved around a subsidy to a tea export company which many members believed, and apparently with good reason, to be a façade.[2] A Hokkaido sugar-beet factory established by six Tokyo men in 1888 with a capital of 400,000 yen was guaranteed by the Hokkaido government a straight 5 per cent dividend on its capital from the month of subscription to the commencement of operations, and thereafter such subsidy as should be necessary to bring net profits (income less costs, less 5 per cent depreciation) up to 5 per cent of capital.[3]

There is a further point to be noted concerning this type of entrepreneurial activity. It was the more effective in that it was able to draw

[1] Furushima and Morita, op. cit., p. 286–7.
[2] *Dai Nihon Teikoku Gikai Shi*, I, pp. 924 ff., 1524–31.
[3] *Shimbun Shūsei*, 7, p. 80.

on established patterns of co-operation. It was reported in 1888, for example, that farmers in Shimane had succeeded in growing an improved type of local cotton, and fourteen of them had established a producers' co-operative (*dōgyō kumiai* on the model provided by the Ministry) to organize spinning and weaving on the putting-out system, and had sent representatives across the country to organize markets.[1]

Enterprise was thus the more effective in that it could be easily channelled into co-operative activity. But while co-operation was traditional, this was a new form. It was not just the co-operation based on ascribed status which prevailed within the solitary village community. It was a new functional and associational form deliberately created, and often cutting across hamlet and village boundaries. Again the State played an important role in providing models for the organization of such groups, model rules not only for the general producers' co-operatives mentioned above, but also for specific types, as, for instance, the model rules for tea-producers' unions circulated in 1883.[2]

Just how much capital investment there was in this type of processing and marketing activity it is difficult to estimate. In terms of the total scale of investments at this time it was probably small. In 1888, for instance, of the 549 new companies established with an average capital of something over 100,000 yen each, only 34, with an average capital of just over 10,000 yen, were designated agricultural.[3] This does not, however, include the small-time producers' union type of investment which was probably greater in its total effect on agricultural production.

It is even more difficult to estimate how much of the total capital invested was urban in origin as in the example of the Hokkaido beet factory quoted above.

Motives of the Innovator

It is time to bring together the various channels of information and pressure towards improvement which have been discussed in a general consideration of the individual innovating farmer. Thousands of farmers in the Meiji period made new departures, did things they had never done before, or did old things in new ways. What were the motives that might have stimulated these innovations? Four are worth considering: a positive hospitality towards novelty as such, as part of a respect for the authority of science and a belief in the possibility and desirability of

[1] *Shimbun Shūsei*, 7, p. 39. [2] *Shimbun Shūsei*, 7, p. 39.
[3] *Shimbun Shūsei*, 7, p. 87.

progress; patriotism; submission to authority; and the calculation of economic interest.

Novelty

That the first was important, particularly in early Meiji, cannot be doubted. It was in a spirit of adventure and experiment that Tsuda bought his farm in Chiba; it was from a missionary zeal for good farming that the ex-samurai, Hayashi Enri, experimented with his premature Lysenko methods of seed treatment and stumped the country giving lectures and distributing pamphlets at his own expense. It was from a desire to catch on to any good new thing that was going that farmers all over the country were stimulated by his pamphlets and his lectures to try his methods themselves. And perhaps when the mass of farmers who could not read pamphlets followed the lead of those who could and did, they too were prompted by something of the same sort of motive. Yanagita Kunio, for instance, had this to say about the farmers he met on lecture tours in 1909.[1] 'When we go to the provinces and talk to the farmers, unless we retail some Western theory we've got out of books or some examples drawn from distant parts of the country, our hearers lack interest and the speaker feels he has not done his job.' Already the 'scientism' which is such a pervasive feature of the mood of modern Japan was apparently well established. It is an attitude which has something in common with American love of gadgetry, but with a difference. Whereas American gadgets are typically conceived as the product of the inventive entrepreneur, Japanese scientism, perhaps because it derives in part from the Confucian respect for learning, looks to the authority of the scholar; there is nothing better than the theory 'got out of books'. Yanagita Kunio has a pertinent point again:[2] 'At the central level administrative authority is always backed by scholarly authority. The top officials are scholars in their own right. And the lower administrative organs feel that if they are retailing their superiors' scholarly opinions as well as their administrative authority they will be all right.' How strong this hospitality to new scientific ideas was among the mass of illiterate farmers in the early Meiji period, and how powerful it was to counter the innate tendency to conservatism of a traditional peasant society, must remain a matter of doubt. What is certain, though, is that the attitude became more powerful as the school system developed and as a new generation of farmers passed through the hands of school teachers

[1] *Jidai to Nōmin*, p. 2.   [2] Ibid., p. 10.

who formed the lower ranks of an intellectual élite in which scientism and the belief in progress was well established. Today, the Japanese farmer is conservative in little more than his politics.

Where this attitude prevails, moreover, social prestige factors give it multiplier effects. The farmer who has a *new* tool acquires prestige thereby and others seek to emulate him. Keeping up with the Joneses has been important to the Japanese farmer not so much in the field of domestic consumption as in the field of ceremonial entertaining and productive equipment. Modern agricultural economists are frequently prone to deplore the abandon with which farmers buy hand-tractors which they can never make economically profitable on their small holdings.

Patriotism

The strength of our second motive is even more difficult to assess. Repeatedly, in the directives of government authority, in the speeches of 'old farmers' at their congresses, in the instructions of landlords to their tenants, rings the refrain 'we must increase production in order to advance the welfare of the nation'. With a nice touch of egotism Yokoi Jikei has his model village mayor place on the wall of the citizens' hall the 'Five Precepts for Farmers' composed by, and inscribed in the bold calligraphy of, Professor Yokoi Jikei. The first reads: 'To increase the wealth of your family is to serve the nation; avoid luxury and always practise diligence.' And the last: 'Understand that farmers must be the nation's model class. Conduct yourself with dignity as befits the heirs of the Bushido tradition.'[1]

Undoubtedly, patriotism, as the highest virtue in the calendar, often served as a respectable, if not hypocritical, cover for other less socially accepted motives. But we should beware of assuming that it was always a cover for economic interest. It could equally serve as a rationalization of the self-assertive adventurism of the samurai rancher, or the missionary egotism of the 'old farmer' innovator. One should equally beware of assuming that it had no independent motivational force at all. Such as it had was probably most marked in the first two decades when there *was* a sense of national emergency. It may be significant that a newspaper writer remarks in 1888 that some time ago it was the fashion for everyone looking for a title for a new company or a new product to use the word *Kokueki*: match factories and beef butchers, all claimed to

[1] *Mohan Chōson*, p. 308.

'profit the nation'. Now, it was remarked, the word is out of fashion. The new cant-word is *Teikoku*; even the sewer man operates an *Imperial Honey Bucket Service*.[1] The magic of the national association is still there, but now reflecting a mood of complacency, latching on to the charisma of established authority, rather than a sense of participation in the striving of a nation trying to pull itself up by its own bootstraps.

Submissiveness

Of our third possible motive enough illustration has already been given. Again we must note that the type of submissiveness that secured obedience to the orders of government, prefecture, mayor or landlord *solely* by virtue of the authority attaching to the latter's superior status became less common as the period went on. The principle that 'the official is noble; the people base' became increasingly irksome as economic opportunity, universal conscription and universal education combined with subversive ideologies to spread egalitarian sentiments.

It was perhaps a reflection of the decline in the absolute authority of the administration that some prefectures resorted after 1890 to the promulgation of by-laws with penal provisions. The objective authority of the law was brought in to bolster declining *personal* authority. In other words, the period of 'extension by the sabre' represented a weakening of authority rather than its intensification as Japanese historians have suggested. And even this did not last long. There was the beginning of articulate and informed opposition. According to one contemporary official reminiscing some fifty years later:[2] 'People argued that it was unconstitutional. . . . If, they said, in order to sell what you have grown you have to submit it to inspection, have it graded and priced according to the grade, and are then forbidden to sell what does not come up to standard, this is a restriction of property rights and an infringement of liberty.'

As the authority of officials declined, so, too, did that of landlords, as the increasing frequency of tenancy disputes after the First World War adequately testifies. But if officials and landlords lost their power to *coerce* by the glare in their eye or by the use of punitive sanctions, they did not thereby lose their power to *influence* provided that they either (*a*) kept the authority relation a warmly paternalistic one, or (*b*) utilized the mechanisms of the solidary village community. The official who

[1] *Shimbun Shūsei*, 7, p. 65.
[2] Ishiguro Tadaatsu, quoted in NNHS, 5, p. 361.

came, not to give orders, but to suggest, advise and guide, 'retailing the scholarly opinions as well as the administrative authority' of his superiors was still respected and welcomed. Indeed, Yanagita Kunio suggests in the same address that there was far too much reliance on the wisdom of authority.[1] 'In future the towns and villages must make greater efforts to study the agricultural economies of their region. The present "leave everything to those above" tendency to welcome the protection and interference of authority is hardly a desirable one.'

By the beginning of the twentieth century paternal government benevolence took an increasingly concrete form – financial subsidies. These began to increase rapidly in amount after the establishment of a network of Agricultural Associations provided channels for their distribution to the cultivating farmer. In 1900 they amounted in total to approximately 1 per cent of the budget of the Ministry of Agriculture and Commerce, about equal to the amount spent on experimental stations. Twelve years later they had quadrupled in amount and were double the size of the experimental budget.[2] And this amount was substantially augmented from prefectural funds.

Wisely used the subsidies were often a valuable spur to useful innovation. And it is worth noting that they were channelled, for the most part, through the Agricultural Associations, and served the secondary purpose of strengthening those organizations which fulfilled our second condition for successful authoritarian guidance.

The importance of this second condition is apparent if one considers the role of the post-war Agricultural Co-operatives, the successors of the old Agricultural Associations. They continue to be a powerful instrument for the execution of government policy and a powerful means whereby the exemplary effects of initiatives by go-ahead farmers can be intensified and accelerated. Their authority derives from the fact that their urgings represent, at least formally, a village consensus, not from the traditional authority of landlord leaders, whom in any case the land reform has removed from the scene.

Economic Interest

The economist, observing the increase in food production in Meiji Japan is apt to conclude that the market provided adequate incentives to encourage farmers to produce more – and by incentives is usually meant a well-sustained price.

[1] *Jidai to Nōmin*, p. 20. [2] NNHS, 5, p. 311.

While it is true that the ability to find a selling outlet for increased production was a necessary condition for the farmer's willingness to produce more, it is doubtful if price levels themselves had much effect on the volume of production. It is unlikely, at any rate, that a typical Japanese farmer's reaction to a fall in the price of his staple products – rice or silk – would be that of the classical entrepreneur – to cut back his investment and the scale of his operations. He was more likely to intensify his efforts to *increase* production – in order to maintain his income by selling more at the lower price. His costs are (*a*) in fact inelastic and (*b*) not usually calculated by him in precise terms in relation to the value of his product.

Generally speaking – though this will be qualified later – the Japanese farmer was production-oriented rather than profit-oriented; or at least he tended automatically to equate production maximization with profit maximization. 'What was good for rice production and what was bad; what was advantageous and what disadvantageous – this was what the farmers most wanted to hear,'[1] remarks Sakawa Jōmei, one of the itinerant lecturers appointed by the Ministry in the 1880s. And whatever the price of rice it was assumed that the more production the greater the profit.

There are, however, two important qualifications which must be entered against this suggestion that the state of the market was irrelevant to the increase in production. The first concerns the matter of fertilizer. Most of the innovations which formed the basis of government urgings did not cost anything. The five 'essentials' enumerated in a central government guide to good cultivation issued in 1903 were, for instance, the selection of seed by the salt-water method; countermeasures for the wheat blight, the use of narrow oblong seedbeds, the use of the seedbed as an ordinary field after transplanting, and the regular planting of rice in rows. No one will ever know just how much these no-extra-cost improvements contributed to the total increase in agricultural production which took place. But it is certain that a great part of the increase is attributable to increased use of commercial fertilizer, not, that is to say, to innovation, but to farmers doing more of what most of them were doing already. The cost of this extra investment *was* something of which the farmer was acutely aware.

It still remains a question, however, how far the current prices for rice directly affected the amount a farmer spent on fertilizer. One's impression (derived from asking altogether over a hundred modern farmers

[1] NNHS, 2, p. 629.

about their use of fertilizer and, as far as I remember, not getting a single answer which related fertilizer cost to the price of rice) is that the use of fertilizer became habitualized. Each increment was absorbed into the farmer's pattern of fixed costs, and if at any time he bought less than the year before this was less likely to be the result of an exact calculation – weighing the probable increment in crop and the probable price of that increment against the extra cost of fertilizer plus interest from spring to autumn – than because he had no cash to buy fertilizer or was so deeply in debt that he feared to extend his credit.

This is certainly the impression one gets from the discussion of the 'old farmers' in 1881. In a long session on different types of fertilizer any number of farmers were prepared to give their views on what was the 'proper' amount of this and that for use with various crops. But only two gave any suggestion of the exact increment in yield to be expected – without any calculation of cost, and only one gave a comparison of the relative costs of two types of fertilizer 'which had the same effect' – without specifying in precise terms what that effect was.[1]

Rice prices did, of course, determine the amount spent on fertilizer, not by affecting incentives, but by affecting the farmer's financial ability to buy it. Even if next year's probable prices had little effect on how much the farmer wanted to spend on fertilizer, last year's prices determined how much he *could* spend.

To sum up, then, as far as rice cultivation is concerned, the economic incentive of increasing production was without doubt a major factor in securing the acceptance of innovations. On the other hand, year to year fluctuations in the market are unlikely to have had any great effect on the volume of production.

Where the market did have its effect was in inducing the substitution of one crop for another. This, however, was almost exclusively within the field of upland agriculture. There was something sacred about the rice-field; it provided the staple of the family's diet, it represented security and it represented years of invested labour in irrigation and other facilities. Even though mulberry and sericulture generally offered a higher monetary yield per acre than rice,[2] it was rare for paddy fields to be turned into mulberry orchards. Crop substitution generally took the form of the replacement of cotton, flax, sugar-cane and millets by mulberry, barley, vegetables and other industrial crops.

The change in crop acreages was considerable. But it came slowly. Even the acreage under mulberry, for instance, the prize example of an

---

[1] NNHS, 1, pp. 755–76.   [2] NNHS, 5, p. 179.

expanding profitable crop, never grew at a rate faster than 5 per cent a year.[1] (On the other hand, the rate of *decline* of clearly unprofitable crops are somewhat faster.[2]) The farmer was cautious, and new ventures were risky. There was nothing comparable to the 'agricultural crazes' – for merino sheep, mulberry trees or Berkshire pigs – which character-ized the United States in the first half of the nineteenth century, or – to take a society more structurally similar to contemporary Japan – to the 'tulipomania' of seventeenth-century Holland. Perhaps the Japanese farmer's love of novelty was not, after all, as well developed as in these societies, perhaps non-official channels of communication were insuffi-cient for these speculative crazes to 'catch on' and develop momentum, or perhaps the Japanese farmer had a more sophisticated awareness of the instabilities of the agricultural market. Yanagita Kunio, again, com-ments in 1909 that there is no lack of bright and enterprising people who are tempted to try something new, to have a go at chicken farming, or start a fruit orchard. But individual decisions cannot take account of the risks of flooding the market. In the natural economy the question 'Why am I poor?' had a simple answer – 'Because you did not work hard enough.' In the commercial economy you can be tough and enterprising – and still lose money. Hence people turn to officials for advice – advice which the officials cannot give for, in all their wisdom, they cannot predict how the market will be in ten years' time.[3]

Even in responding to market inducements, in other words, farmers tended readily to seek official guidance. They also, frequently, sought psychological security and marketing convenience in a collective response. It was probably as common for a group of farmers to start something new as for one to start individually.

The way in which farmers' contacts were made with the market is a complex question, worth exploring in the context of urban-rural rela-tions. Sometimes, again, officials were the mediators – as in the case of the conversion to mulberry in Shimane to which the tenants objected. In the early period the major role was doubtless played by individual merchants. But not all of these were urban-based merchants. The rural merchant-farmer, whose importance in the late Tokugawa period has recently been described by T. C. Smith, was doubtless of considerable importance. Later, as the Agricultural Associations became organized, they began to go half-way to meet and even create opportunities – energetic leaders in the Association would seek arrangements with factories for the purchase of industrial crops. At a later stage came

[1] NNHS, 5, p. 180.   [2] NNHS, 5, p. 174.   [3] *Jidai to Nōmin*, p. 10.

collective marketing operated by the Association itself or by co-operatives. Unfortunately, there is no way of making a quantitative assessment of the relative importance of merchant enterprise and farmer initiative in catalysing the crop substitutions which contributed an important part to the growth of agricultural productivity in the period.

The Old and the New: Rural and Urban

In the foregoing discussion the main emphasis has been on the mixture of the old and the new in the factors which promoted the expansion of agriculture in nineteenth-century Japan. Important continuities with the Tokugawa period were pointed out; the Confucian tradition that 'agriculture is the base of the country' as a partial explanation of Government concern with agricultural policy; the – again originally Confucian – respect for learning which gave a traditional means whereby innovation could be legitimized as an application of scholarly theory, and whereby those who sought to induce improvements could invest themselves with authority; the tradition of the literate, carefully recording, sometimes consciously experimenting 'old farmer'; the tradition of peasant submission to political authority which permitted improvement by fiat; the tradition of paternalistic patron-client relations between landlord and tenant which permitted the 'old farmer' type of landlord to exert a guiding control; and finally the tradition of community solidarity and community homogeneity which required individual submission to the constraint of village rules and village opinion which it was open to innovators to manipulate.

These elements, with the exception of the first which was an attitude of the already 'urban' samurai, were features of the rural tradition which facilitated agricultural improvement from within, sometimes operated even to initiate it, and in any case to magnify the effects of stimuli applied from without. Much of the stimuli did, of course, come from without – from the urban sector: the technology, flowing at first from the West and later increasingly from home experimental centres, channelled through the urban agricultural colleges and the urban centres of government; perhaps, in relatively small amounts, urban capital flowing into food processing industries; the new mass education system with its urban origin and – as men like Yokoi Jikei were apt to complain[1] – its excessively urban orientation, sharpening receptivity to change and providing new motivations; and finally the economic inducements

[1] Shakai Seisaku Gakki, *Shakai Seisaku Ronsō*, no. 8 (1915) pp. 64-5.

presented to the farmer by the urban-based merchant. These elements of the urban new combined effectively with the rural old. New wine in old bottles is the cliché that comes immediately to mind, an inapt one since it cannot accommodate the fact that the bottles responded extraordinarily well.

5 Agriculture and economic development in Africa: theory and experience 1880–1914

C. M. ELLIOTT

I

'The role of agriculture in economic development' has a strangely foreign ring in Africa. In a continent in which the urban employed population is tiny, in which only a small proportion of the population derive their living directly from non-agricultural sources, the development of agriculture is almost synonymous with economic development. As *per capita* income rises, import substitutive industries may provide a small industrial base, which may be further extended by agro-allied industries. But until intermediate demand has grown to a level sufficient to support a nascent capital goods industry, the bulk of the population must rely upon increasing agricultural output for an improvement in the standard of living. Even at quite high average *per capita* income figures, this may imply, for many individual farmers, a transition from subsistence to semi-commercial or full commercial production. In the period with which we shall be primarily concerned in this essay, namely 1880–1914, the connection between economic development and agriculture was inevitably so close as to be identical. Although cultural contact was very much older, the heyday of colonial rule was just beginning and with it, in European circles, dreams of agricultural wealth abounded. If the heroes of such dreams were sometimes planters and settlers, administrative policy soon recognized the practical and political problems that would attend large-scale alienation of land. Thus in West Africa almost exclusively, and in East Africa to a very considerable extent (except in the White Highlands of Kenya), agricultural development devolved upon the local population. But official interest in the development of African agriculture was motivated less by dreams of empire than by the mundane necessities, first, of creating a taxable income within the territory; second, of creating demand for expensive transport systems, the prime object of which was to serve administration; and third, of producing agricultural goods, and particularly, of course, cotton, for the industries of the metropolis.

In the absence of even the guidelines of a comprehensive history of agricultural development, it would be presumptuous to try, in the space allotted here, to write on so general a theme as that implicit in this volume. Accordingly, the object of this paper is more modest. In the first part we develop a general theory of agricultural production, which attempts to take a little further work already done in this field. In the second part we examine our model against the experience of four African countries – Ghana and Sierra Leone in West Africa; Kenya and Uganda in East Africa. The treatments of these countries do not pretend to be full economic histories, but illustrations of the way in which the variables included in the model appear to have operated, and thus some guide to the explanation of significant and interesting variations in experience.

II

It is perhaps worth emphasizing that the model that will be briefly out-lined in this first section does not pretend to be an operational model. It is designed to serve a descriptive purpose of specifying as accurately as possible certain important relationships, and setting within one analytical framework variables which have sometimes been mentioned in the literature but which have never been adequately related to each other.

The basic starting-point in any analysis of African agriculture must be labour. Within the period under discussion capital goods were usually of the most simple variety, and were in most cases the direct product of the farmer's own labour. Typically though not universally land was abundant, and the process of bringing land into cultivation, whether temporarily or permanently, was labour intensive. Thus before we can analyse satisfactorily changes in output we must first ask about changes in labour input. The basic economic question therefore is, how does the farmer distribute his available resource, namely labour, in such a way as to maximize his welfare? Before attempting to answer these questions it is necessary fully to appreciate the significance of leisure in most traditional African societies. Leisure is not merely the absence of work, a vacuous residual which betokens a large reservoir of potential labour. This primitive view, the unimaginative product of cross-cultural trans-ference, has survived too long in much economic literature. Detailed studies of how farmers actually spend their time, particularly in seasons in which the demand for agricultural labour is lower, reveal that although they may then be economically unproductive they are socially at their most productive, maintaining kinship bonds, giving and receiving status gifts, transacting legal proceedings, and generally servicing the intricate fabric of their society. This social expenditure of labour time has, of course, an economic product, in so far as in many tribes farmers are dependent upon labour from relatives and clan relations for help in the harvest. But that is a subsidiary issue in the sense that social bonds are maintained for their own ends and not for economic purposes. Any discussion of 'labour abundant economies' must be heavily qualified by the awareness that the labour abundance is in some ways more apparent than real. A simplistic calculation that relates total labour time productively employed to total labour time potentially available oversimplifies the time commitments of the individual farmer. A high leisure preference does not necessarily imply idleness. Nor does it necessarily imply the more liberal interpretations of idleness, as a result of ill health, malnutrition or deficient motivation. Leisure may be accorded a high preference because without it the bonds of society would atrophy and the whole social organization would thus disintegrate.

In our terms we can thus say that the individual farmer's utility function will accord a high marginal utility to at least a substantial portion of leisure time. This fact, plus the seasonality of many African crops, together with their time-sensitivity,[1] can give rise to a labour shortage at certain times of the year, even in so-called labour abundant economies. To this extent, as we shall emphasize later, the labour input can be a real constraint on production, even though in aggregate terms the marginal productivity of labour may be low. Apart, then, from adequate leisure to fulfil his social obligations, the individual farmer also requires output for subsistence; cash for the payment of taxes or other long-term inescapable commitments; and a sufficient surplus to indulge in what may be termed subsistence trade, e.g. the purchase of a wife or wives.[2] These are not choices, but necessities, and therefore the question

---

[1] By time-sensitivity we mean that yields fall unless specific operations are performed at the right time. Thus maize yields have been found to be very responsive to planting at the correct time, with rapid falls in yields if planting is long delayed.

[2] In Central Africa there is some evidence that the rate of increase of agricultural output is directly correlated with the rate of divorce. If a man divorces his wife, he may not get the bride-price back, or if he does it will usually be over a long period. In the meantime he will almost certainly wish to remarry, which will entail at least a down-payment on his new wife. Cf. Polly Hill, *The Cocoa Farmers of Ghana* (Cambridge, 1963).

of allocation hardly applies to them. In addition to these necessities the farmer would like to have income to buy goods, the urgency of this desire being related to a number of variables to which we shall return. We can thus distinguish two cases. In the first, the desire to buy goods, either directly through participation in the monetary economy or indirectly through some involved system of barter, will be so small that all the farmer's needs including cash for unavoidable commitments, and leisure, can be met. In this case the necessity to substitute one good for another does not arise. This we may call the crude subsistence case. The other case is where the demand for income conflicts with the demand for leisure. Depending upon tribal patterns and particularly the prevalence of superstition attaching to wealth, the possibility of substitution may in fact be quite limited.

However, it is quite misleading to think, as for instance Szereszewski seems to do,[1] in terms of a pure choice between income and leisure. No less fundamental is the fact of risk. In broad terms, the poorer the cultivator and the less perfect the social security offered by the extended family system, the more serious is the result of a miscalculation of risk. The marginal utility of risklessness is not functionally related to income, precisely because of the insurance offered by the extended family and other social organizations. But in both the pure subsistence and incipient commercial cases, the risklessness of a farming plan is quite as important as its demands for labour and its potential yield. It is not only the case that a farm plan with too high a risk element entails the possibility of starvation for the family (in a tribal and clan society, individual, as opposed to corporate, starvation is a rarity, even in bad years). In some ways more significant is the fact that failure of a new crop opens the cultivator to the ridicule of his peers, and therefore brings an important loss of status. But these social factors in the assessment and acceptance of risk can work in both directions. As we shall see in relation to the cotton revolution in Uganda, social pressures can be brought to bear upon producers, which by introducing social risk into the situation reduces the utility of economic risklessness in relation to the other variables. Personality factors may well enter here too. There is no reason to believe that *ceteris paribus* different personalities will react to a risk situation in the same way. Further, as we shall mention below, the actual assessment of risk will of course differ from individual to individual.

The welfare maximizer will therefore wish to equate the marginal

[1] R. Szereszewski, *Structural Changes in the Economy of Ghana 1891–1911* (London, 1964).

utilities of income, leisure and risklessness, and equilibrium will be where

1. $mu_y = mu_r = mu_z$
   where y = income, r = risk and z = leisure.

The supply of labour forthcoming, then, is determined by the relationship between the individual farmer's preferences for leisure, income and risklessness on the one hand and on the other the work, risk and yield constellation of given cropping patterns on the other.

There are thus different types of constraint acting on the farmer's output. First, the constellation of demands of leisure, income and risklessness of a given crop may exceed the farmer's readiness to meet those demands. Let us assume, for instance, that the farmer has a relatively low utility for income but a high utility for leisure and risklessness. An export cash crop will give him ample income in return for a large input of work and the acceptance of considerable risk, since the opportunity cost of growing the crop is not only leisure but also the cultivation of other (food) crops. Under these circumstances – a paradigm of the pure subsistence case – the farmer will rationally refuse to produce the export crop. A substantial improvement in his terms of trade, brought about by an increase in the price of the crop and/or a cheapening of goods (since income is only an intermediate good) will induce him to grow the crop only if the increase in total utility from higher income thereby offsets the loss in utility furnished by higher risk and increased work. The effect of changes in the terms of trade are therefore determined by the relative strengths of the other two variables. If, on the other hand, income has a high relative marginal utility, there will be less resistance to new cropping patterns and the effect of changes in the terms of trade will be proportionately greater.[1]

It thus becomes important to establish the factors that determine the relative marginal utilities of leisure, income and risk. We have already said enough about the social importance of leisure in the tribal economy to be able to conclude that for any individual the marginal utility of leisure will depend not only upon the amount of work performed, but also upon his social status within the clan group (which will determine the amount of time which he is socially obliged to spend on such activities as attending court, meetings of elders, consulting with the

---

[1] But some allowance must be made for the increasing social risk of greater wealth. This constitutes a feedback element which will to some extent offset the high relative marginal utility of income.

Chief and so forth), the social arrangements of his particular clan, the geographical mobility of his clan, and the degree of dispersion of his extended family (if long journeys are required to maintain kinship bonds this is clearly more time-consuming and therefore leisure-demanding than if the family and clan group are in one closely defined area) and the necessity to indulge in non-productive tribal activities such as war, hunting or forced labour for the Paramount Chief or sub-Chief. Again it must be emphasized that these activities were not, in the period under discussion, alternatives to settled farming or the growing of export crops. It is the latter that were optional extras; the former were social and to a lesser extent economic obligations placed upon the individual, to be ignored at his considerable peril.

The determinants of the marginal utility of income, at least in developed countries, are fairly well known. They include such factors as the absolute level of income, the rate of change of income, the level of committed (e.g. in our case, taxes and school fees) in relation to total income, the size of the family and past income peaks. For traditional African societies none of these can be dismissed out of hand, but there are two additional related factors which perhaps have a greater effect on determining the marginal utility of income. The first is the development of the retail sector. The impact of the rural retail sector has received far too little attention from development economists and economic historians. In it we include not only the establishment of retail outlets on the European or Asian patterns, but also, as will become evident in the next two sections, the activities of indigenous traders. The rural retail system has a wide variety of effects, of which the most important are, first, a demonstration effect, creating desires for goods that have hitherto been non-existent. Gin, firearms, 'American' cloth, ironmongery and enamelware were the precursors of today's bicycles, transistors, watches and factory-made furniture. In general, the exhibition of these goods was enough to arouse a desire to own them. This was enhanced by the second effect, namely that of making available to a wide range of potential consumers the goods under discussion. As internal trade routes improved, and in some cases superseded long trans-Saharan caravans, so the range of goods actually available to the consumer improved. To this extent it is true to say that effective supply created at first latent demand and then effective demand. The third effect of the development of the rural retail system is the encouragement it gave to the determination of status by the ownership of bought goods. In traditional societies status is determined by many variables, such as age, skill in witchcraft,

ability in war, reputation for wise counsel and family, and the superses-
sion of these status determinants by the ownership of bought goods was
neither quick nor complete. None the less, even by 1900 the ability to
clothe oneself in imported fabrics was accepted as a mark of status; and
the ownership of a gun, with all its quasi-magical powers, was a most
significant social differential. These three services rendered by the
development of rural retailing, however defined, were most important in
creating a desire for imports and therefore a demand for cash.

This demand for cash we may call a transactions motive. The other
important motive was precautionary. Particularly among those farmers
whose standard of living had already developed beyond that of subsistence, i.e. who were already dependent upon bought goods to some
extent, the need arose for cash reserves to act as contracyclical resources
in times of bad harvest. Quite apart from variations in the prices of
crops, such uncontrollable factors as irregularities of climate, incidence
of disease and untimely variations in the family's available labour force
ensured that output and hence income were highly volatile. Particularly
when long-term commitments such as school fees and to a lesser extent
of course taxes had been accepted, there was a need to expend cash
holdings to guard against years of disaster. That this suggests a fairly
high average propensity to save on behalf of quasi-commercial farmers
should occasion no surprise. Although it is entirely true that social
pressures were brought upon relatively wealthy farmers to share their
wealth with the clan group, these obligations were not entirely incon-
sistent with savings, since in years of famine or crop failure the whole
clan group would have access to the cash resources of the wealthier
members.

We have already touched upon the determinants of the utility of risklessness – the size of family, the articulation of the clan and extended
family systems, the level of income and the rate of change of income (if
any) and perhaps the most important the competence with which the
individual farmer could assess the risks involved. This depended upon
the nature of the risks, the distribution of probabilities. The greater the
variance of rainfall, the greater the possibility that a given risk assessment will be wrong, and therefore the greater is the utility to be derived
from avoiding that particular risk.[1]

If these, then, in summary form are the principal determinants of the
marginal utilities of the three variables under consideration, we can see

[1] See Michael Lipton, 'The Theory of the Optimising Peasant', *Journal of
Development Studies*, June 1968.

that a whole host of social and economic factors will determine the reaction of an individual farmer to a given economic stimulus. More particularly, they will determine the relative strengths of the income and substitution effect following, for instance, an improvement in the farmer's terms of trade. For instance, the more the retail system is developed, the greater is the demand for cash in the rural areas; and the higher the past income peaks the more ready will the producer be to substitute in come for leisure, i.e. the greater will be the substitution effect in relation to the income effect following an improvement in the internal terms of trade. This excess of the substitution effect over the income effect will be further increased if the extended family system is such that the farmer can spread the risks of his enterprise amongst his kinsmen. In general, the extent to which labour is terms-of-trade-elastic is determined by the degree to which the demand for cash offsets the demand for risklessness and the demand for leisure. Where, for a given cropping pattern, the required work and risk are too high in relation to the potential income, the farmer will never willingly adopt that cropping pattern.[1]

The other type of constraint that may operate can be mentioned more quickly. It may be that a given crop demands a greater input of, let us say, risk and labour than a farmer has available. Let us concentrate again on the labour constraint. Under what conditions will the individual farmer start hiring labour and using it to supplement family labour? The availability of labour for hire implies, first, a shortage of land, since we assume that most farmers would prefer to produce for themselves rather than accept positions of wage labour. Second, it implies the fact that the extended family system has been adapted in such a way as requires the able-bodied to work rather than exist at subsistence level upon the earnings of their clansmen. Or, conversely, it may imply that for some individuals the marginal utility of income exceeds the marginal utility of leisure. They are, therefore, prepared to substitute leisure for income by accepting positions as wage labourers. The demand for wage labour implies one of two things. First, it may imply that the employer prefers to substitute leisure for income, and therefore substitutes incomes and risk (since wages imply a commitment of income) for income. Or, secondly, it may imply such a high marginal utility of income that the employer substitutes leisure and risk for income. In a society in which

[1] In terms of equation 8 in the Appendix where the partial derivatives of leisure and income approach zero, the production plane and the indifference plane may never in fact be tangential. In this case there is no possibility of the farmer producing the crop and remaining in a position of indifference to his former position.

the demand for cash and income goods is high, therefore, and in which there is a net shortage of land, we would expect to find the beginnings of a rural proletariat, whose employers themselves work.

The tacit assumption of welfare economics, that the individual welfare maximizer can consciously and accurately make a series of decisions which will result in the achievement of his goals, is doubly dubious in the context of traditional agriculture. In other words, it takes a certain amount of technical knowledge and managerial skill to arrive at the combination of income, leisure and risk that is indeed preferred above all others. There is thus no necessary identity between the preferred income/risk/leisure combination and the achieved income/risk/leisure combination. This is obviously true in relation to risk, since a farmer may badly miscalculate the risk involved in a given cropping pattern. But it is hardly less true of income and leisure, since a farmer may intend to reduce leisure and increase income but then find that he has badly miscalculated the revenue to be realized from a given crop or the work input required for a given crop. Indeed, one of the elements of the whole concept of risk is precisely that the preferred point within the preference space may be badly over- or under-shot.

To summarize the discussion so far, we have suggested that the terms-of-trade-elasticity of labour supply in traditional African agriculture is determined by a whole range of social and economic variables, which may be conveniently summarized by the notion of the marginal rates of substitution of leisure for income for risk. In broad terms, the higher the demand for cash, and the less strong the extended family system, and the less demanding the social organization in terms of time for social functions, the greater the income effect is likely to be in relation to the substitution effect. In the analysis that follows we shall initially merely refer to the elasticity of labour as a given constant, though by making elasticity a constant we may well be oversimplifying the picture in so far as the determinants of elasticity are variables themselves, and may change quite quickly once the other variables that we consider in the next paragraphs begin to change significantly. This oversimplification does not critically affect the analysis, though clearly it should be borne in mind when applying the ideas behind the model to a given historical case.

In the Appendix a formal production function is developed; here we merely discuss the nature of the variables and the crude relationships between them. Output is assumed to be the result of labour – directly and indirectly – in the sense that labour creates farm-land and capital. The marginal productivities of labour in these three uses are therefore key variables in explaining the growth of output. Clearly, the marginal productivities of land and capital must also themselves be taken into account. Further, there is an allocative choice involving decisions on whether to invest labour – on capital or land production – or to use it directly on existing assets. The farmer's ability to make this choice will depend upon his managerial ability. Further, his capability as a manager will, to a large extent, determine the yield he achieves from a given set of inputs. The managerial ability to *get organized* in peasant farming is a much under-emphasized variable, particularly since the time-sensitivity of crops has such a substantial impact on yields. Managerial ability in this sense will depend, not only upon the education (perhaps), psychology and social circumstances of the individual farmer, but also the complexity, newness and scale of his farm pattern. In the formal model in the Appendix we explore how output grows over time with these variables and then introduce changes in the supply of labour resulting from both the elapse of time (i.e. changes in population) and changes in the terms of trade.

Taking these variables together, we can see that variations in output are determined by the following likely sequence of shocks to an equilibrial system. As a result of the factors discussed above, the supply of labour becomes more elastic, thus increasing the supply of labour at a given level of the internal terms of trade. If the terms of trade of the farmer simultaneously improve, perhaps as a result of increased transport facilities, the supply of labour increases further. The additional labour supply is productive on the existing stock of other factors but, according to the managerial ability of farmers, new assets are created and as they become productive, so output rises further. It would be possible to build a response-lag into the model so that output would rise in discontinuities as first labour was applied to existing resources and then new resources came into production. In some cases – e.g. cocoa – these lags would be quite long. Both the effectiveness with which new assets are created, and their productivity when brought into production, depend upon the productivity of labour which is applied to them. In part this will be influenced by exogenous factors such as technical progress imported from abroad, and in part by endogenous transformations of work patterns brought about, for instance, by population pressure.

We must now consider the determinants of the level and rate of change of the marginal productivities of labour in its various uses and of capital and labour. Clearly they are not entirely independent since the same level of technology and rate of technical progress will apply to all three – e.g. clearing and cultivation will be done with the same class of tool, be it axe, machete and hoe, oxen or tractor. At the same time, they may be complementary. For instance, under conditions of increasing population pressure, if new land is scarce or unobtainable (so that the marginal productivity of labour in land-clearing is low or zero), simple diminishing returns theory suggests that unless it is possible to substitute capital for land (i.e. intensify agriculture) the marginal productivity of labour will begin to fall. This process is, of course, well documented.[1] It is a fair stricture of our model as so far developed that it does not readily take account of technical progress – clearly the basic determinant of all the marginal productivities since it assumes that all capital is labour-created and therefore does not adequately treat of imported capital goods in which technical progress may be embodied – ploughs, insecticides or tractors. To take account of this objection, we may adopt the crude technique of including a variable of imported capital, which we may assume exogenously determined. It will in fact depend upon a whole host of variables, probably the most important of which is government expenditure on extension services and the supply and quality[2] of credit available in the rural areas.

Apart from capital imports and the rate of growth of population, there are two other sources of technical progress which deserve fuller discussion than they can be given here. First is the development of an enclave economy with its attendant infrastructure and employment opportunities. The former, especially railways, have the most obvious and immediate effect on the terms of trade by reducing the cost of imports and increasing the value of exports.[3] But they also have the effect of reducing the amount of labour involved in the marketing process and thus free labour for either more productive employment or the enjoyment of more leisure. Alternative employment opportunities can have two opposing effects. Gulliver, for instance, comments on:

> the fact that the returned labourer with his stock of money savings and clothing tends to feel that there is no compulsion for him to work immediately after getting back home. He has perhaps enough clothing to last nearly a year and cash to buy further clothes and pay his tax in

[1] W. Allan, *African Husbandman* (Edinburgh, 1965); R. J. M. Swynnerton, *A Plan for the Intensification of Peasant Agriculture in Kenya* (Nairobi, 1958); E. Boserup, *Conditions for Agricultural Progress* (London, 1965).

[2] In the sense of rates of repayment and interest and security demanded.

[3] We assume that the marketing structure is such that these effects are in fact passed on to the producer.

the following year. . . . Thus many men merely help in normal food production and leave cash crops until savings are considerably reduced or entirely spent.[1]

On the other hand, the transmission of cash from the money economy to the rural sector can act as a savings pool for investment in productive assets – e.g. by supporting a man while he brings land under cultivation. Although less well documented, this effect is likely to have been growing as the relative size of the money economy has increased.

III

In this section we use the model to compare and contrast the experience of Uganda and Kenya – particularly the Northern Province of Kenya – in the establishment of cotton as a cash crop. The period 1904-10 poses the interesting question of why the reaction of African farmers in Uganda to the introduction of cotton was more positive than the reaction of farmers in Kenya. Given in broad terms the similarity ecologically and climatically, and the same political environment following the annexation of East Africa by Britain, it might be expected that the reaction of the Buganda and, for instance, the Luo in Kenya would be very similar. However, whereas the export of cotton from Uganda had reached £50,000 a year by 1908, the crop had almost ceased to be grown in Kenya. Whereas in West Africa (to a greater extent amongst the Yoruba than on the Gold Coast) the part played by non-indigenous forces, except for the initial introduction of the crop, had been small, in East Africa the administration had to struggle hard to get the crop accepted and established at all. From the administration's point of view the crop was attractive. Partly owing to naïvely enthusiastic accounts of the terrain of East Africa the colonial government did not expect the administration of the country to be a charge on the metropolitan revenues for very long.[2] It was therefore necessary to extend the cash base in order to generate sufficient African holdings of cash for the payment of taxes. The hut tax, for instance, was introduced into Uganda in 1900 with the intention of initiating the process of taxing the local population. Great difficulty and substantial losses were reported when

---

[1] P. H. Gulliver, 'Labour Migration in a Rural Economy', *East African Studies*, no. 6 (1955) pp. 35-6; reprinted in E. H. Whetham and J. I. Currie, *Readings in the Applied Economics of Africa*, I (Cambridge, 1967) pp. 35-6.

[2] *The Times*, 1 October 1892, quoted in C. Ehrlich, 'The Economy of Buganda 1893-1903', *Uganda Journal*, XX (1956) p. 18.

Africans insisted upon paying their taxes in kind. And the administrative attempts to substitute a *corvée* system for payments in kind were only partially successful. If the major objective of policy, namely to encourage the protectorates to become financially self-sufficient, was to be achieved it was clearly necessary to increase the quantity of cash in the hands of the African population. Since there were no alternative employment opportunities, in contrast for instance to mining on the Gold Coast in roughly the same period, and copper mining in Northern Rhodesia after the First World War, the only possible source of cash revenue for the African farmer was the cultivation of cash crops.

Four other factors influenced both the timing of the introduction of cotton and the choice of that crop as the main income earner for the African farmer. The first was the need to generate traffic for the Uganda railway, finished in 1901. The railway was built more for administrative convenience than as a realistic commercial undertaking,[1] but having invested £5½ million in its construction the colonial government found it necessary to attempt to generate traffic for it.[2] The similarity with the Lagos–Kano railway is clear. But when this latter railway failed to generate the supply of cotton that the British Cotton Growers' Association had expected, it was more than ever desirable that East Africa should produce the commodity which West Africa had signally failed to deliver. With the uncertainty in terms of both availability and price of American lint the British cotton manufacturers were doubly anxious to find alternative cheap sources of supply.[3] Fourthly, the conviction persisted that the colonies could provide a large and growing market for British manufactures, if they were once provided with the means of earning an adequate income.

All these factors were common to both countries. The colonial administration expected a rapid development of cotton production from both countries. The interesting question therefore is, why was this hope fulfilled in Uganda but confounded in Kenya?

In terms of our theoretical discussion, we must consider the development of the rural retail sector, the demand for cash, past peak incomes and the risk factor. We start with the risk factor, since there can be little

[1] But see D. A. Low, 'British Public Opinion and the Uganda Question, 1892', *Uganda Journal*, XVIII (1954).

[2] See, for instance, H. Fearn, 'Cotton Production in the Nyanza Province of Kenya Colony, 1908–1954', *The Empire Cotton Growing Review*, XXXIII (1956) p. 123; C. C. Wrigley, 'Crops and Wealth in Uganda', *East African Studies*, no. 12 (1959) p. 13.

[3] See the King's Speech of 1904, quoted in W. O. Henderson, *The Lancashire Cotton Famine*, Manchester, 1934.

doubt that this element played a considerable and perhaps even decisive part in the initial reluctance of the Luo to grow cotton. Not only was it a new crop, requiring hard work (e.g. careful weeding) and worse, accurate timing of work (i.e. harvesting when the cotton boll was at precisely the right stage of development), but also lack of experience with the crop made it impossible for the farmer to appreciate the probability of returns from this unusual degree of effort. So much was common to both the Buganda and the Luo, but whereas the location chosen for the initial development of the crop in Uganda was entirely suitable both ecologically and climatically, the same could not be said for the location chosen in Kenya for the development of cotton-growing by the Luo. In Kenya the administration introduced cotton on the lake-side plateau where the rainfall was highly variable and on average only barely adequate for the growing of this crop. Ignorance of the crop would require a high risk premium in both locations, but in Kenya the variation in rainfall meant that the probability of that premium being met was low. Thus the more rational was the farmer's approach to cotton-growing the less likely was it that in Kenya he would in fact become an established grower.

The relative disinclination of the rational farmer in Kenya to grow cotton was increased by the fact that in Kenya the opportunity cost of growing cotton was growing food, and was especially high in years when the main rains failed; the bulk of the family's food had to be grown during the short rains. Since the Luo grew crops with high labour-demand peaks such as maize, the competition between crops for family labour at sowing and weeding times, and to a lesser extent at harvest, was intense. It was therefore a perfectly rational reaction to give cotton a low priority in the allocation of available labour. But since cotton is highly sensitive to weed competition, this inevitably resulted in low yields and therefore low returns. In a situation in which the farmer was trying to limit his risks, the employment of immigrant labour would clearly have been most inappropriate.

Now, exactly the opposite was the case with the Buganda. These people depended for their subsistence on an easily grown, low labour input crop, namely plantain. 'Food production was so sure and easy that it could be relegated to the background of life and left almost entirely to the women of the tribe.'[1] Therefore the Buganda did not

---

[1] C. C. Wrigley, 'Buganda: An Outline Economic History', *Economic History Review*, 2nd ser., X (1957) p. 71. Contrast for the Kavirondo of North Nyanza, Günter Wagner, *The Bantu of North Kavirondo*, II (Oxford, 1956) pp. 20 ff.

regard cotton as a competitor to their main subsistence food. As they were thus able to devote the time required to the cultivation of cotton, the probabilities of a paying crop were thus increased, and the employment of immigrant labour thus represented a much smaller degree of risk. In Buganda 'a total failure of the crop was virtually inconceivable'.[1] To the extent, then, that rainfall was less regular in Kenya and that the opportunity cost of growing cotton was lower in Uganda, the risk element was clearly lower in Uganda than it was in Kenya.

The next factor to be considered is the demand for cash. Clearly since tax regulations applied with equal force to both areas there is little difference in the demand for cash for taxation. The main variable, therefore, is the demand for cash for the purchase of imported goods. Immediately one important factor becomes relevant. The Luo were a non-hierarchical people, and thus lacked the wealth of social distinction which was a characteristic of the Buganda. There can be little doubt of the effect of social hierarchy upon the needs and aspirations of consumers. Broadly speaking, it is surely true that the more hierarchically-differentiated a people, the more likely it is that the demonstration effect will operate. This is particularly the case when gift giving and receiving is an important part of relationship formation. One can thus detect the same difference between the Luo of Nyanza and the Buganda as one can between the Hausa Fulani of Northern Nigeria and the Ibos of Eastern Nigeria. There is, however, a further important distinction which has an equal bearing upon consumption patterns. The Luo were traditionally a cattle-keeping people, and therefore were basically a migrant tribe, following their cattle to new grazing as the seasons demanded. The opposite, of course, was true of the Buganda, basically an agricultural people living in settled villages. The important difference then was between the migrant life of the Luo, which militated against the building of permanent houses, and the hierarchical settled existence of the Buganda, which implied a much more permanent form of settlement, and therefore a higher standard of housing.[2] The role of housing as a determinant of consumer patterns in Africa has been as yet little explored, but there can be small doubt that it is a most important factor, affecting the range and level of consumer demand of the family. A settled existence and a permanent dwelling make desirable goods and

[1] Wrigley, 'Crops and Wealth', op. cit., p. 15.
[2] 'As early as 1893 the "prime minister" was dispensing judgement in a two storey brick house with the aid of a battery of clerks.' Wrigley, 'Economic History', op. cit., p. 74. See too Wrigley, 'Crops and Wealth', op. cit., p. 17, and refs. there quoted.

K 2

chattels which a migrant, living in a temporary hut, would regard more as encumbrance than convenience. For both these reasons, then, it is at least highly probable that the demand for cash for the purchase of imported goods was higher among the Buganda than it was among the Luo. Obviously we have no statistical measure of such differences, but it may well be significant that the Asian traders who followed the development of the Uganda railway did a much livelier trade in Uganda than they seem to have done in Nyanza.[1]

It is difficult to use constructively the concept of management with a people so recently emerging from a totally traditional environment. However, the concept of hierarchical differentiation may again be important in so far as it is usually thought to operate as a constraint on efficient management. The argument usually is that as the society is hierarchical, it is also traditional, and is therefore opposed to the creation of new values which efficient management usually implies. This is obviously an oversimplification, since there are examples of hierarchical societies which have produced extremely efficient managers – the Hausa and the Yoruba in Nigeria are sufficient examples. Equally it could well be argued that the need to maintain a hierarchy is itself an incentive towards a more efficient distribution of both economic and political resources. Certainly the historian of the Ganda concludes that their 'society was acquisitive and competitive to a degree unparalleled in East or Central Africa'.[2] Further, not only were the chiefs better educated – among them illiteracy had almost disappeared by the turn of the century – but also the tribesmen were better disciplined and technically more competent, thanks in large part to the establishment by the C.M.S. of a technical school.

Additionally it could be argued that since it was the task of the women to produce food among the Ganda and of the men to serve at court, and particularly to make war, the creation of the *pax Britannica* implied a degree of unemployment among the Ganda tribesmen. Put another way, the demand for leisure fell and there was surplus labour

---

[1] For the rapid development of retail trade in Uganda after the completion of the railway, see Ehrlich, loc. cit., pp. 20–1. But prior to that the demand for goods was evidently sluggish. A C.M.S. missionary complained that 'owing to the incoming of the Europeans a new market has been formed and old people can now sell what was unsaleable before and can get much better prices. Their requirements have not kept pace with the better payment for labour, therefore the people can supply all their simple wants with a small amount of labour and spend the rest of their time in idleness.' Quoted from C.M.S. archives, ibid., p. 23.

[2] Wrigley, 'Economic History', op. cit., p. 73.

capacity which required a lower return to enter productive employment. Certainly it is significant that when the price to the grower began to fall in 1907, largely as a result of deterioration in the quality of the crop, the reaction of the Luo was to stop growing the crop while that of the Ganda was to grow more of it – thus implying quite different supply curves.

So far, then, we have shown that the Ganda were more likely than the Luo to substitute leisure and risk for income. We now come to a consideration of changes in the terms of trade. Clearly the opening of the Uganda railway, with its terminus at Kisumu on the Nyanza shore of Lake Victoria, marked a discontinuity in the internal terms of trade for farmers in both Nyanza and Buganda. Hitherto the only means of transport of output away from these territories, and imports into them, was by native porters bearing headloads. There is plenty of evidence of how expensive this form of transport was, particularly in relation to the rates that the railway were able to offer. From our point of view the important question is the difference in the terms of trade between Nyanza and Uganda. The key point is that the effect of the railway on the most distant parts of the Nyanza province was less than the effect of the railway on the coastal areas of Buganda. The latter were connected to Kisumu by the efficient lake transport organized by the Arabs, but the former were still dependent on native bearers for transport to Kisumu. The contrast, then, is not between Nyanza, which had the railway, and Uganda, which did not, but between those parts of Nyanza which were immediately served by the railway and those parts of Buganda which were served by the lake extension of the railway on the one hand and the more distant outlying areas of both territories.

The crucial role of the provision of transport was well appreciated by the contemporary Governor of Uganda, Sir H. Hesketh Bell, who wrote:

> Satisfactory as the progress of the past four years has been, the further extension of the industry on a scale commensurate with the possibilities of the country will mainly, if not entirely, depend on the provision of transport facilities. Up to the present the cultivation of cotton has been restricted to the districts that lie within a moderate distance of the ports on the shore of Lake Victoria. The native of Uganda is very willing to grow cotton, or, indeed, any other product which fetches a reasonable price, but he detests having to carry his crop to market, on his head, over a long distance. A journey of thirty to forty miles is the outside limit that he is willing to travel with a load of his own produce. A radius of forty miles from a market may be

taken as the extreme limit of area of profitable production under existing conditions.[1]

For this reason he gave the development of road transport a high priority, particularly in areas well suited to cotton. Lacking such a feeder system, in Nyanza the effect of the railway was very much more circumscribed.

Of the other variables in the model, we can easily discuss only one, namely the import of capital. Apart from the railway, which we need not discuss further, the most important capital import was the extension effort of the administration. As we have already stressed, the introduction of cotton as a crop originated with the administration. 'This year we are confining our efforts to Kano and Kajulu, where *twenty-five loads of seed* have been issued. I hope by working a small area, and thus being in a position to exercise constant supervision, to get most of the seed planted, and what is more important, to keep the plots clean afterwards.'[2] The extension effort and the distribution of free seed were common to both areas, but the energy and generosity with which the policy was pursued were greater in Uganda, particularly after 1908,[3] than they were in Kenya. More particularly in Uganda the chiefs were persuaded of the desirability of growing cotton and it was they who acted as extension officers:

> So far, with the exception of a single experiment on a small scale by a European planter, the cultivation of cotton in Uganda has lain entirely in the hands of the natives. Profitable though the industry soon proved itself to be, the average peasant of the Protectorate is so naturally indolent that it is unlikely that he would have embarked on it on any considerable scale if he had not been more or less driven to making experiments by the chief or headman on whose land he happened to be a tenant [sic]. It may be acknowledged that, in most cases, the peasants made their first ventures almost under compulsion. The results of the first crop, however, rendered further pressure unnecessary. The native who hitherto had found it a matter of considerable difficulty to provide himself with the means of paying his rent and taxes, soon realized that even a very small field of cotton would give

[1] *Report on the Introduction and Establishment of the Cotton Industry in the Uganda Protectorate*, Cd 4910 (1909) p. 12.

[2] District Commissioner's Report 1910–11. Quoted by H. Fearn, *An African Economy: A Study of the Economic Development of the Nyanza Province of Kenya, 1903–1953* (Oxford, 1961) p. 68.

[3] Wrigley, 'Crops and Wealth', op. cit., p. 15.

a yield in cash exceeding his greatest hopes; plots of cotton sprang up all over the country, and an almost unlimited spread of the industry has been checked by the lack of transport facilities alone.[1]

Together with the Uganda Company, the colonial administration developed a satisfactory relationship with the chiefs that ensured that improved seed was used[2] and that the way was open for, in Hesketh Bell's phrase, 'timely help and guidance'.

IV

Our second case-study is concerned with West Africa in the same period. In Nigeria, Ghana and Sierra Leone palm oil and, particularly in the case of Sierra Leone, ground-nuts were the principal agricultural exports in the period 1860–80. By 1910, Ghana and Western Nigeria had experienced the cocoa revolution and Sierra Leone had greatly expanded her production of palm oil and kernels. In this brief review of these developments we shall first discuss the features common to Ghana and Sierra Leone which account for the rapid agricultural development in this period, and then consider the more difficult question of why Ghana went out of palm-oil production into cocoa, while Sierra Leone expanded the former at a time of falling world prices.

There can be little doubt that the development of the retail sector in West Africa had reached a considerable degree of sophistication by the period under consideration. Writing in 1893, for instance, Sir William Brandford Griffith had this to say:

> There is further in this colony a vast and almost inexhaustible field for what is known as the petty trader, semi-educated men who, purchasing small quantities of dry goods and other articles saleable to the natives of the interior, carry them to the inland towns and villages and either sell them or barter them for rubber, palm kernels, monkey skins or other marketable exports, and so turn over their money twice to great advantage as a rule to themselves.[3]

In Yorubaland the development of an internal market was no less far advanced and the fact that Lagos had been one of the principal entrepôts

[1] Bell: Cd 4910 op. cit., pp. 10–11.
[2] The mixture of seed became a serious threat to the crop by 1908. Hence the necessity of controlling the quality of the seed planted.
[3] Quoted in Polly Hill, *Migrant Cocoa Farmers of Southern Ghana* (Cambridge, 1963) p. 165.

in the slave trade gave to the hinterland a special degree of sophistication in retailing.[1]

At much the same time, and in much the same terms as Brandford Griffith had written of the traders of the Gold Coast, Rowe wrote to Sir Michael Hicks-Beach of Sierra Leone:

> The genius of the Sierra Leone people is commercial: from baby-hood the Aku girl is a trader, and as she grows up she carries her small wares wherever she can go with safety. The farther she goes from the European trading depots, the better is her market. These people do more than collect the native produce, they stimulate its cultivation. Many bushels of palm kernels are collected by the native women, and then they buy the handkerchief and the looking-glass brought to their village by the Sierra Leone adventuress. If she never visited them, those kernels would have been left to rot on the ground. Tons of Kolah are exported from Sierra Leone which would have never been gathered from the trees had not this pushing huckster found her way inland. . . . I think I am not exaggerating when I say that nine-tenths of the kolah nuts shipped from Sierra Leone are collected by Sierra Leone traders in districts outside the settlement. . . . [The travelling traders'] presence in a country or their being driven away from it directly influences the sale there of British manufactures and the export of African produce.[2]

From this it seems reasonable to conclude that the development of the retail sector was fairly advanced even in the remoter areas of West Africa.[3]

From that it does not necessarily follow, however, that the demand for cash was the same. There are two important differences. First, as Polly Hill has emphasized, the expansion of cocoa-growing in the Gold Coast was dependent upon the sale and purchase of land by the cocoa growers. More particularly, a cardinal point in her treatment of the growth of cocoa production is the fact that this land was paid for by instalments. Although a contemporary account of land sales makes it clear that if the vendee fails to maintain his repayments the vendor has no power to sell

[1] See K. Onwuka Dike, *Trade and Politics in the Niger Delta, 1830–1885* (Oxford, 1956) pp. 203 ff.

[2] Quoted in N. A. Cox-George, *Finance and Development in West Africa* (London, 1961) p. 149n.

[3] For a most interesting account of the trade routes in the hinterland of Sierra Leone, see P. K. Mitchell, 'Trade Routes of the early Sierra Leone Protectorate', *Sierra Leone Studies*, N.S. 16, June 1962.

the land to anyone else but must wait for his money, there was none the less considerable pressure upon the vendee to complete the transaction in order that the expansion of his cocoa lands might be continued.[1]

In Sierra Leone the proclamation of a protectorate over the hinterland in 1896 necessitated an immediate increase in the public revenue. This was made the more urgent by the cession to France of large parts of the hinterland which had hitherto been served through Freetown, thus contributing substantially to the lucrative export taxes. By 1898 the Administrator had assured the Colonial Secretary that he 'had under consideration the important question of stimulating the production of exportable articles in the Protectorate. . . . The loss in export trade caused by Freetown ceasing to be a depot for the rivers and territory now under French administration can be more than compensated by the development of the Natural Resources of the Protectorate.'[2] These factors led directly to the introduction of a hut tax by the Protectorate Ordinance of 1896, which, as modified after the Hut Tax War by the Ordinance of 1901, fixed a flat rate of five shillings per hut, and interestingly made the chiefs the collecting agents. This put considerable pressure on the chiefs, since in the opinion of Sir David Chalmers, who was appointed Royal Commissioner after the Hut Tax War, the amount of tax was higher than the people, taken generally, could pay. The chiefs therefore had to make up the deficit out of their own funds. Contemporary commentators concluded that the chiefs were being forced into permanent and cumulative debt.[3] We may thus conclude that in Sierra Leone the demand for cash, taken with the development of the retail sector, ensured that the pressures making for a high rate of substitution of income for leisure were considerable.

In so far as past peak incomes may influence leisure/income preference patterns, it is relevant that in the palm-growing countries incomes from this source were falling fast. The price of palm oil fell 22 per cent from 1890 to 1913, and in the Gold Coast, for instance, production fell from over 4 million gallons per annum in the mid-1890s to barely more than three-quarters of a million by 1913. Palm-oil producers therefore were faced with falling real and money incomes (since there is no evidence of a simultaneous offsetting fall in import prices) and if the peak income effect operates at all, we would expect it to operate in those circumstances.

These then were the factors making for an increase in the amount of

[1] Hill, op. cit., pp. 142, 182. [2] Quoted in Mitchell, loc. cit., p. 208.
[3] Cox-George, op. cit., p. 75.

143

labour forthcoming. Their effect was dramatic. In his penetrating mono-
graph, Szereszewski has computed:

> an increase in the labour intake of the cocoa industry from about
> 100,000 labour days in 1891 to 37,000,000 in 1911, together with a
> marked increase in the very labour intensive distribution connected
> with the export and import trade, and an export record of the other
> agricultural commodities which does not imply clear reductions in
> labour intake . . . should suffice to indicate that the core region of the
> economy . . . did increase to a very large extent the supply of labour
> services to activities included in the G.D.P. Since the rate of popula-
> tion increase was low, *per capita* labour services must also have
> increased.[1]

Here is ample demonstration of the multiplicative effect of an increased
labour-supply elasticity and an improvement in the farmer's terms of
trade following a switch from palm oil (falling prices) to cocoa (high and
initially rising prices).

Risk in cocoa-growing is inherently high since the gestation period is
so long. Further, in the period with which we are concerned, cocoa was
a new crop of which the vast majority of the population had had no
direct experience. And indeed the early history of the crop in the Gold
Coast had done little to inspire confidence. Yet among the Akwapim of
the Gold Coast and the Yoruba of Western Nigeria this high risk does
not seem to have acted as a deterrent. Partly this can be explained in
terms of higher education and a more rational attitude to risk; partly by
social structure, perhaps particularly among the basically urban Yoruba;
and partly by the fact that the crop does not interfere unduly with the
production of food-crops, and in later years positively encourages it.

Indirect or ambiguous though the relationship may be, the management factor is none the less related to education. If we take management
in its wider sense, so that it includes not only managerial ability to make
circumscribed optimizing decisions but also the ability to absorb and
implement new technical possibilities, then it is fairly clear that in the
Gold Coast, and to a lesser extent in Yorubaland, the educational status of
at least the important elements in the community was considerably higher
than that of the inhabitants of Sierra Leone. The work of the Basle Mission in this connection has already been much emphasized,[2] and certainly
it is significant that the technical training provided by the Basle Mission

[1] Szereszewski, op. cit., p. 75.
[2] Szereszewski, op. cit., pp. 7–9, 21; Hill, op. cit., pp. 170–2.

produced not only a surplus of skilled artisans, many of whom emigrated, but also a more general awareness of the possibilities of technical change.

This was almost totally lacking in Sierra Leone, so that Risely Griffiths, writing in 1881, could complain that 'the native implements are still of the rudest kind; their hoes are little more than sufficient to scratch the ground, and their only other implement a cutlass to cut down the bush. Ploughs are unknown and spades are little used.'[1] Government efforts to induce technical change were confined to laudable, if mildly laughable, attempts by individual governors to emulate nineteenth-century country gentry in founding agricultural and botanical societies, and it was not until 1895 that there was an officially established post for an agricultural expert. The local administration does not seem to have practised the energetic policy of agricultural improvement that was followed in East Africa, and although the founding of a Department of Agriculture in Sierra Leone preceded that in Kenya by twelve years, the energy with which it implemented its policies left much to be desired, at least until 1911. Thus although Lemberg, for instance, could write of 'millions of acres of rich and fertile soil which the railway would make accessible to the energy and enterprise of hundreds of people, who would become extensive and profitable growers of coffee, cotton, indigo, cocoa, and numerous other tropical articles which are in constant demand in commerce', and could see 'Sierra Leone being reckoned in a few years among the great coffee and sugar producing countries of the world', these dreams of 1888 were never fully realized.[2]

This technical inferiority largely explains why cocoa was not grown in Sierra Leone. It was introduced into the colony before 1896 and was readily available in that year in Freetown from the Government Botanical Station.[3] Although it would be rash to dogmatize, further factors may explain why Sierra Leone never shared in the cocoa boom. First it is doubtful whether the crop would have prospered with sufficient certainty and regularity in Sierra Leone's climate to have minimized the risk involved for peasant producers. In other words, given that cocoa is, in some ways, an inherently high-risk crop, conditions must be ideal for its physical welfare for it to be readily adopted by peasant producers. Sierra Leone is neither wet nor humid enough for cocoa to flourish

[1] T. Risely Griffiths, 'Sierra Leone, Past, Present and Future', *Journal of the Royal African Society*, quoted in Cox-George, op. cit., p. 135.

[2] Quoted in H. H. Lardner, *Manual on Cultivation and Preparation of Tropical Crops* (London, 1890) p. 91.

[3] H. D. Tindall, 'Early Introduction and Cultivation of Economic and Ornamental Plants in Sierra Leone', *Sierra Leone Studies*, N.S. 9 (1957) p. 50.

generally and it therefore represents a high risk.[1] Second, government seems to have made little attempt to encourage the cultivation of the crop. In the Gold Coast, by contrast, the Director of Agriculture advertised the crop with enthusiasm: 'I strongly recommend all planters with suitable land to start cocoa planting without delay, as I am convinced that the low prices which are now being paid for palm oil, kernels and coffee do not fully compensate them for the large amount of labour which the preparation of these crops entail.'[2] By the time Sierra Leone had organization and enthusiasm to match those of the Gold Coast the peak of the cocoa boom was past. Third, around Freetown and in the original colony, land was in short supply, and for liberated Africans settled in the colony the land tenure question was so uncertain and vexatious that serious involvement in long-run agricultural investment was unattractive. Further, with the rapid growth of Freetown and its environs, food prices were high and rising, thus making it more profitable, especially in the short- and medium-runs, to grow rice and other foodstuffs to supply to the non-agricultural population.[3]

Last and most important, there is some evidence to suggest that the role of the railway from Freetown to the lands of the Mende in the south-east of Sierra Leone was crucial. The railway was floated on dreams of agricultural development and indeed its only *raison d'être* apart from administrative convenience, was to tap the resources of this potentially rich source of supply. Although served by ancient trade routes, the Mende had failed to take adequate advantage of them since the bulk/value ratio of much agricultural produce was unfavourable. However, once the railway penetrated this area, the production of palm kernels soared – by over 70 per cent in the first decade. The suggestion is that the improvement in the terms of trade brought by the railway was adequate to offset the fall in the price of palm products, and thus gave no stimulus to substitute a high risk, little known crop for one that was well-tried and no less profitable than hitherto. Indeed, given the transport economies effected by railways elsewhere it would be surprising if there were not a net gain in the farmers' terms of trade and therefore an incentive effect to continue to produce palm oil and kernels. The fact that it was possible to reach a new income/leisure/risk equilibrium is further attested by the scarcity of wage-labour in Freetown by the end of the first decade of the century. Inevitably explained by the 'inherent

---

[1] But it seems to have flourished along the seaboard of Sherbro, perhaps from very early times. See W. Hopkins, 'Agriculture in Sierra Leone', *Journal of the African Society*, XIV (1914–15) pp. 145–6.

[2] Quoted in Szereszewski, op. cit., p. 83.   [3] Hopkins, loc. cit.

apathy of the natives',[1] it is more probable that the wage rates paid by government and private employers did not compete with the incomes available to successful palm-oil producers.

V

In conclusion, we have tried to demonstrate some of the factors which determined agricultural development – or the lack of it – in four African countries at the beginning of this century. In Ghana, Buganda, and to a lesser extent Sierra Leone, agricultural progress and therefore economic growth were dependent upon a massive increase in labour inputs. This resulted from improved terms of trade, better technologies (i.e. new crops) and a greater readiness to substitute income for leisure. But wherever a substantial increase in risk was involved in this transformation, as with cotton in Kenya and cocoa in Sierra Leone, agricultural development proved impossible in the period under review. We have also tried to bring out the role of education, and particularly technical education, as a necessary precondition of rapid agrarian progress. It is surely not entirely coincidental that the Basle Mission and the C.M.S.-backed Uganda Company were both deeply involved in the initiation of the two agricultural revolutions we have reviewed: nor that both had been concerned with technical training over a period of time before the introduction of the new crops.[2] The other major variable which seems to have been active was the import of capital through railways and government extension effort. But this was a necessary, not a sufficient, condition of development, as is suggested by the experience of Kenya, where it was present, and Sierra Leone, where it was absent. The wider question of the long-run effect of this capital import upon economic development calls into question the glib equation between agricultural progress and economic development that we have assumed throughout this treatment. But that would take us way beyond the scope of this essay.

MATHEMATICAL APPENDIX

1. *The Supply of Labour*
In the main text we saw that the supply of labour forthcoming is determined by the farmer's preference for his three maximands and technical

---

[1] Hopkins, op. cit., p. 147.

[2] As a matter of detail the Uganda Company was not formed until 1903, but its work in this connection had begun as an 'industrial mission' out of which the Company grew. See C. Ehrlich, *The Uganda Company: The First Fifty Years* (Kampala, 1953) pp. 4 ff.

characteristics of the crop (or crops). Formally this can be put in terms of a familiar utility surface, defined in a space of which z, y and r are the coordinates. We define the marginal rates of substitution as

$$(1)\ S_1 = \left(-\frac{dy}{dz}\right) r \text{ constant}$$

$$(2)\ S_2 = \left(-\frac{dy}{dr}\right) z \text{ constant}$$

and we assume that there are no discontinuities in the partial derivatives.

$$(3)\ \frac{dy}{y} = S_1\left(-\frac{dz}{z}\right) + S_2\left(-\frac{dr}{r}\right)$$

will define the indifference plane upon which changes in risk, labour and income leave the farmer indifferent.

If

$$(4)\ \frac{dy}{y} + S_1\left(\frac{dz}{z}\right) + S_2\left(\frac{dr}{r}\right) = 0,$$

then it can be shown that the gradients of the plane so specified are determined by the ratios of the functions S_1 and S_2. Further, the differential equations

$$(5)\ \frac{dy}{1} = \frac{dz}{S_1} = \frac{dr}{S_2}$$

give a tangent direction, perpendicular to the above plane and specified by S_1 and S_2. Only if (4) is integrable can we specify an orthogonal system, but since we have assumed no discontinuities in the partial derivatives, we are assured of a system of curves from (5) whether or not (4) produces a system of indifferences surfaces; (5) therefore specifies a set of optimum expansion 'paths' which, simplified as

$$(6)\ dy = \frac{S_1}{S_2},$$

merely states that an optimal expansion 'path' for a small increment in leisure is defined by the ratios of marginal rates of substitution of leisure for income and risk. For any given value of y therefore there is a unique set of increases which the farmer prefers above all others, and which in the case of (4) being integrable, will increase his welfare at the most rapid rate.

148

Now the three dimensional equivalent of the budget line or isocost curve we shall call the iso-revenue/risk plane. This is specified by the total differential, which may be stated in the form

$$(7) \frac{dy}{y} = \frac{\delta y}{\delta z} \, dz + \frac{\delta y}{\delta r} \, dr$$

Only when the farmer's expansion 'path' approaches consistency with the iso-revenue/risk plane of the cropping pattern is labour likely to be made available for rapid expansion.

2. *The Production Function*

We start with the simple assumption that output is a function of labour and its average productivity. That is

(8) $V = aL$, where V is output,

a is average labour productivity in direct production,

L is labour used in production.

Since land and capital also enter into production, however, and since labour is used to create them, we can say

(9) $\Delta K = \beta(L)$.

(10) $\Delta N = \gamma(L)$, where ΔK is the increase in the capital stock ΔN is the increase in land in use.[1]

Output is then the sum of aL and the marginal productivities of new capital and land.

(11) $V = aL + \pi(\beta L) + \varrho(\gamma L)$ where π is the marginal productivity of capital,

β is the marginal productivity of labour in capital creation,

ϱ is the marginal productivity of land, and

γ is the marginal productivity of labour in land clearing.

But since there is an allocative choice about the resources to be devoted

---

[1] Not necessarily arable. Grazing land may need some improvement – e.g. eradication of poisonous weeds, digging of wells.

to the production of land and capital, it is necessary to introduce a management factor, M. This refers to the physical ability to choose and implement a given range of factor inputs and, *pace* Johnson's objections, is a variable that must be included in the production function. In the following equation, then, M refers to the managerial ability of the farmer and σ to the responsiveness of output to changes in that ability.

$$(12) \quad V = aL + \pi(\beta L) + \varrho(\gamma L) + \sigma(M)$$

may be differentiated with respect to time to give

$$(13) \quad \frac{\mathrm{d}V}{\mathrm{d}t} = \left(a\frac{\mathrm{d}L}{\mathrm{d}t} + L\frac{\mathrm{d}a}{\mathrm{d}t}\right)\frac{\delta V}{\delta L}\frac{\mathrm{d}L}{\mathrm{d}t} +$$

$$\left(\pi\beta\frac{\mathrm{d}L}{\mathrm{d}t} + \pi L\frac{\mathrm{d}\beta}{\mathrm{d}t} + \beta L\frac{\mathrm{d}T}{\mathrm{d}V}\right)\frac{\delta V}{\delta L}\frac{\mathrm{d}L}{\mathrm{d}t} +$$

$$\left(\varrho\gamma\frac{\mathrm{d}L}{\mathrm{d}t} + \varrho L\frac{\mathrm{d}\gamma}{\mathrm{d}t} + \gamma L\frac{\mathrm{d}\varrho}{\mathrm{d}t}\right)\frac{\delta V}{\delta L}\frac{\mathrm{d}L}{\mathrm{d}t} +$$

$$\left(\sigma\frac{\mathrm{d}M}{\mathrm{d}t} + M\frac{\mathrm{d}\sigma}{\mathrm{d}t}\right)\frac{\delta V}{\delta M}\frac{\mathrm{d}M}{\mathrm{d}t}$$

If we assume that the variables in Greek script are time invariant, the form of the equation becomes

$$(14) \quad \frac{\mathrm{d}V}{\mathrm{d}t} = (a + \pi\beta + \varrho\gamma)\frac{\delta V}{\delta L}\frac{\mathrm{d}L}{\mathrm{d}t} + \sigma\frac{\delta V}{\delta M}\frac{\mathrm{d}M}{\mathrm{d}t}$$

To take account of the importation of capital we need only add to (13) the further expression,

$$\left(\mu\frac{\mathrm{d}Km}{\mathrm{d}t} + \frac{Km\mathrm{d}\mu}{\mathrm{d}t}\right)\frac{\delta V}{\delta Km}\frac{\mathrm{d}Km}{\mathrm{d}t}$$

As we have already mentioned, the supply of labour is determined by the elasticity of labour with respect to the internal terms of trade.

$$(15) \quad \frac{\mathrm{d}L}{\mathrm{d}T} = \frac{L}{T}\cdot\frac{1}{\eta}$$ where η is the elasticity of labour supply: T is the terms of trade,

and

$$(16) \quad \frac{\mathrm{d}^2L}{\mathrm{d}T\mathrm{d}t} = \frac{T\eta\left(\frac{\mathrm{d}L}{\mathrm{d}t}\right) - L\left(\eta\frac{\mathrm{d}T}{\mathrm{d}t} + T\frac{\mathrm{d}\eta}{\mathrm{d}t}\right)}{\dfrac{\mathrm{d}t}{(T\eta)^2}}$$

6 Mexican agrarian reform 1910–1960

RAYMOND CARR

In the growth stakes Mexico is a star performer: since 1940 there has been, on average, a growth rate of 6 per cent without serious inflation after 1954.[1] This is, in Latin America, a quite exceptional achievement. So rapid has been the growth of industry that the term 'industrial revolution' has been used to describe it. Moreover, agricultural production has risen at the same time as industrial production; indeed the *rate* of agricultural growth has exceeded that of the United States and Canada at their maximum.

How far is this impressive agricultural growth connected with agrarian reform in the sense of redistribution and the *ejidal* system? How far has agricultural reform been a condition of industrial growth? Unfortunately, no clear answer is possible,[2] largely because the Mexican Revolution, which began in 1910 and is still considered by Mexicans a continuing and unfinished process, was a complex phenomenon of which agrarian reform was only one, although one of the most important elements.

As far as the agricultural sector is concerned the concentration on *growth* is in itself deceptive, since it tends to obscure the low base from which growth starts, though this argument applies less the nearer we come to the present day. The Revolution itself was an agent of enormous destruction in the years 1913–24, so much so that agricultural production did not recover its 1910 levels until the late 1930s, and between 1921 and 1929 it probably declined 11 per cent; in 1930 the *per capita* production of the staple food, maize, was the lowest in Mexican history. Revolutionary destruction had affected the transport system, the marketing system, and there was great physical destruction and neglect of irrigation systems.[3]

---

[1] See Table I, p. 167.

[2] This is also the conclusion of the recent work of G. C. Cumberland; see his *Mexico* (New York, 1968) especially p. 303.

[3] Only those products for which there was a very strong international demand escaped, e.g. henequen in Yucatán, where, in any case, there was less fighting than, say, in the centre and north and less dependence, for instance, on long haul rail transport.

Even given this reservation, the overall performance of the Mexican economy since the 1940s remains impressive; but it is precisely here that the variables become so complex. The Revolution, for instance, created a strong sense of national purpose which verged on xenophobia; it gave the executive the power of a dictatorship, but a dictatorship with a popular base. It was this unchallenged executive power which could create the instruments to force industrial growth: a successful system of import licensing, a sophisticated system of state-encouraged industrial investment, a control of labour that could dampen the wage-cost spiral. Above all, as far as agriculture is concerned, it provided a dose of infra-structural investment in irrigation, which no other Latin American country could match – partly because elsewhere so much investment went into middle-class housing or social welfare, and perhaps because no comparably dramatic extension of cultivable land by irrigation was possible, or considered possible, in other countries.[1] Apart from these factors, which can be deduced, as it were, from the Revolution, Mexico enjoys other advantages: nearness to the United States market for certain agricultural crops, and special treatment for capital goods imports by the United States during the Second World War – a period which corresponded to a critical stage in industrialization[2] – an income from tourism which helps to alleviate the constriction on imports.

Nevertheless, it is the assumption of many Mexican economists, for instance Edmundo Flores, that the income redistributive effects of agrarian reform without compensation are an essential part of Mexico's success.[3] Others argue in more general terms: the destruction by agrarian reform of a dominant unenterprising class of large landholders and its replacement by a 'dynamic' middle class. No longer does the railway run for 125 kilometres through one estate. 'The former estate owners', writes González Navarro, 'have turned into dynamic and active

---

[1] It is important to realize that investment in irrigation, far from implying general investment in agriculture, was made at the expense of such general investment. In 1939–59 investment in irrigation totalled 7·4 billion pesos; investment in agriculture generally 1·1 billion.

[2] The parallel with Perón's Argentina is instructive; even with available foreign exchange Argentina could not industrialize after 1945 because capital goods were in short supply on the world market.

[3] Flores argues the case in his *Tratado de Economia agrícola* (Mexico, 1961). In 'On financing Land Reform: A Mexican Casebook' in *Studies in Comparative International Development*, iii, no. 6 (Washington University, St Louis), he shows how the Mexican government achieved redistribution of income and eluded its obligations to compensate for expropriation.

businessmen.'[1] At the other end of the scale, even amongst the poorer *ejiditarios*, old ways of life are in question. The effects of *bracero* emigration to the United States are sometimes dramatic, and Belshaw has shown the decline, through increased contact with the world outside the village, of such supposed foundations of the Mexican rural character as *machismo*.[2]

The argument that agrarian reform achieved in the name of the Revolution after 1915 was and is an essential precondition of growth turns on an interpretation of Mexican agrarian history and on a model of the latifundio system.

Mexican agrarian history is seen as a struggle between the free land-holding 'Indian' village and the hacienda or over-large, extensively cultivated estate.[3] The hacienda system, with its roots in colonial Mexico, was enormously strengthened in the nineteenth century, especially in the later years of the rule of Porfirio Díaz – the authoritarian ruler overthrown by the Revolution in 1910 – and especially in the north and south of the country. Its expansion took place at the expense of the Indian village lands, not so much because the *hacendados* wanted land as because they wished to monopolize labour. In Chevalier's telling phrase, the haciendas, after the appalling decline in population that followed the Spanish conquest, were an empty frame that must be filled with labour. 'We must not allow the poor to have their own cornfields,' says a post-revolutionary *cacique*, 'because then they will work for us.'[4] The expansion of the latifundio was stopped short in 1910; instead the revolutionary governments fostered, at varying rates, the establishment of the modernized village community – the *ejido*.

Now it is the universal verdict that the latifundio was responsible not merely for agricultural stagnation but for a climate hostile to industrial enterprise. It was the attitude of the hacendado which was so inimical to 'healthy' growth: they were satisfied with low returns on capital, they were reluctant to modernize or to produce for the market. The classic denunciation of the hacienda was written shortly before the Revolution by Molina Enríquez: 'An Hacienda is not a business', it was based on

[1] N. González Navarro, 'Mexico: The Lop-Sided Revolution', in C. Veliz, *Obstacles to Change in Latin America* (London, 1965) pp. 206 ff.

[2] M. Belshaw, *A Village Economy. Land and People of Huecorio* (New York, 1967). *Machismo* is the behaviour demanded of the virile, self-confident, dominant male.

[3] This is the historical theme of E. N. Simpson's classic *The Ejido. Mexico's Way Out* (Chapel Hill, 1937).

[4] In Oscar Lewis, *Pedro Martínez* (New York, 1964) p. 7.

'a spirit of domination', not on profit. No race of entrepreneurs could spring from such unpromising soil. This verdict has been continuously reinforced: for instance, Pérez López, a director of commercial policy, writes, 'the latifundium is not adapted to the need to produce an agricultural surplus'.[1] The standard structuralist argument emphasizes the resultant inelasticity of food supply and consequent diminishing import capacity together with inflation.

No one would now attempt to defend the latifundium or to deny the capacity of a latifundio system to distort an economy; it has always been what the eighteenth century called an *estorbo*, an impediment to growth. The problem is to find the classical latifundium, described for instance by Tannenbaum, *when alternatives are available* which will allow the *latifundistas* to behave more rationally.[2] Some models, at least, seem to contain two contradictory assumptions:

(*a*) Latifundistas are conspicuous spenders, living lives of luxury in Mexico City, if not in Paris. Presumably, therefore, they are interested in profits made from marketing *outside* the hacienda. The first generation of revolutionary novelists turned such idlers into a fictional stereotype.

(*b*) The hacienda is directed primarily towards internal self-sufficiency, not external profits, though clearly a minimum of external profit is necessary. Its instrument is a labour force tied to the soil – either by debt-peonage or a small amount of land in return for service – together with a seasonal labour force of *minifundistas* who cannot live on the produce of their plots and must seek outside work.[3]

I would like to suggest that, because of the growth of a significant rich 'bourgeoisie' with expensive habits during the late Díaz period, the largely self-sufficient old-fashioned hacienda was no longer socially rewarding, just as Russian landowners found that the adoption of European tastes made the simple patriarchal life impossible. What inhibited the commercialization of the hacienda was not merely the lack

---

[1] See Molina Enríquez, *Los grandes problemas nacionales* (Mexico, 1909) pp. 84 ff., and Enrique Pérez López, 'The National Product of Mexico', in *Mexico's Recent Economic Growth* (Latin American Monographs, University of Texas, no. 10) p. 24.

[2] For Tannenbaum's description see his 'Toward an appreciation of Latin America', in *The United States and Latin America* (New York, 1963) pp. 29 ff.

[3] Of course in part this is due to the fact that both types do exist. The typical local landed potentate or *gamonal* of Upper Peru (described by F. Bourricaud in *Poder y sociedad en el Perú contemporáneo* (Buenos Aires, 1967) pp. 22 ff.) represents type (*b*); the Morelos sugar hacienda type (*a*).

154

of inclination or even, perhaps, the incapacity to make profits, but high transport costs. With inadequate transport, self-sufficiency was not an aim, it was a necessity; investment was irrational. When in the 1840s Fanny Calderón de la Barca asked an *hacendado* why he did not irrigate his land and produce for the market, he replied 'that from this estate to Mexico [City] the distance is thirty-six leagues, that a load of wheat costs one real a league . . . so that it would bring no profit if sent there'. In a Mexico dependent on mule trains, the railway investment of Díaz opened the first opportunity for commercialization:[1] this happened soon with alcoholic drinks and cotton. Once the railway reached Torreón, the 'classic' hacienda disappeared under a wave of new investment: before 1910 Torreón was the most rapidly growing town in Mexico. Hence the 'stable' hacienda was under pressure. It was not the old, semi-self-sufficient, hacienda which produced pre-revolutionary tensions, but the commercialized sugar haciendas of Morelos, and in the north, where the effects of U.S. and other investments were beginning to be felt. It was not immemorial injustice but the irruption, after the 1890s, of a new race of profit seekers. Conservative peasants have usually as great an interest in traditional systems as conservative landlords; it is the landlords' attempts to modernize which cause revolt.[2]

The pre-eminence of the classic hacienda was being eroded not merely by economic progress but by intellectual criticism. One of the most curious features of the nineteenth century is the persistence of a belief in the uneconomic nature of large property and in the necessity for smaller properties and a fluid market in land as a foundation for liberalism. This was one of the basic tenets – perhaps derived via contemporary Spanish legislation against entail – of the liberalism of the *Reforma* of the 1850s.[3] Even Díaz's *científicos* were beginning to question the economic value of the over-large hacienda, not least because of its inability to supply cheap food for an expanding market. Needless to say,

[1] For the old transport system and its costs see D. Cosío Villegas (ed.), *Historia moderna de México*, VII (Mexico, 1965) p. 772.

[2] This is true, for instance, in southern Peru where attempts to introduce blood stock entailed wiring and limitation of the grazing rights that went with the 'traditional' hacienda. Chevalier has pointed out how Morelos, with its heavy Indian population, was turned into a centre of revolt when traditional landlords sold out to sugar capitalists. Zapata, the figurehead of Mexican agrarian reform, came from Morelos and, indeed was interested in little else but conditions there (cf. F. Chevalier, 'Le soulèvement de Zapata', *Annales*, XVI (1961) p. 66).

[3] These views are well set out in Silva Herzog, *El Agrarismo Mexicano y la Reforma Agraria* (2nd ed., Mexico City, 1964).

neither the liberals nor the *cientificos* were willing to envisage expropriation as a basic step for a more liberal or efficient structure of landownership.[1]

As has been frequently pointed out – indeed with a certain glee by the left – the only result of the liberal reforms of the nineteenth century was further to threaten the landholding Indian villages without creating a race of small proprietors.[2] Indeed it was to give the legal foundation for the enlargement of the hacienda at the expense of the village.

Only by appreciating this failure can we understand the legal structure of land reform in Mexico. Once liberal reform flung communal land into the open market and stripped it of its traditional legal protection, the small landholder – a sort of yeoman farmer to be created by liberal legislation – became the victim of the large landholder. The mechanism is well known: debts, crop failures, etc., forcing sale to those who are economically powerful enough to resist the consequences of a bad year and indeed to profit by them. Obregón, the first revolutionary President to take land reform seriously, saw that the large landowners must be destroyed if the small landholder was to survive.[3] Because the whole history of the nineteenth century showed the dangers of the open market to the small man, the whole aim of agrarian reform in Mexico after 1910 was to take the peasant plot *out* of the market – to make it inalienable, above all unmortgageable. This was the whole purpose of the *ejido*, the central instrument of agrarian reform after the Revolution. The land was the peasant's as long as he cultivated it; he could not alienate it. Simple knowledge of what had gone on in Mexican history from the days when indebted *caciques* sold village lands to Spanish landowners led to a return to Aztec practices. Neither *indigenismo* nor socialism was responsible.

With the decree of 6 January 1915 the leader of the Constitutionalists, Carranza, accepted the principle that land of which they had been

[1] Private property was especially protected by Article 27 of the liberal constitution of 1857.

[2] The 1856 law was intended to convert communal holding into individual holdings. In my view the language of the law threatening communal property was as vague as the language protecting the *ejidal* holdings. In any case, the real onslaught on communal lands, using the 1856 legislation, came in the 1890s when the Indians were forced to convert their holdings into freehold. The 1856 law was directed primarily against church holdings but involved other corporate landholders, e.g. the Indian villages.

[3] At least in theory. The 1924 Reglamento aimed at creating stable small property without imperilling economically productive larger units. This may be taken as the continuing purpose of Mexican land reform; it has never been directed against 'small property' but against overlarge holdings. The difficulty is to find out what is meant by 'small property'.

despoiled should be restored to communities, and that if no process of restitution was possible, then land should be expropriated from adjacent holdings to ensure the 'well-being and development' and to give land 'to the miserable rural population'. The decree was vague – Carranza, as his record shows, was no zealot for distributive reform – but together with the primacy of public interest over private interest established in the constitution of 1917 it provided the foundation for all subsequent legislation.[1] From it later came the *ejido* which created communities of peasants whose affairs were regulated by an elected committee, whose plots could not be alienated, and which could be cultivated either collectively or individually. It is important to realize that the legislation of the Mexican Revolution – the Revolution to Mexicans is a continuing process – did not attack private property as such. Indeed Article 27 of the constitution specifically protected 'small' private property in land: the identified enemy of the public interest was the large landowner. Thus the Mexican Revolution created a dual system: the *ejidal* sector and a private sector consisting, supposedly, of 'small' property.

Why was Mexican land reform such a slow process? We have already explained the sheer physical destruction. It must also be remembered that agrarian reform is a complex and *legally* technical and difficult process. Mexicans in 1915 had no example of *how* to set about land reform: thus reformers had little realization of the connection between land reform and credit facilities and agricultural education.[2]

Above all, the early stages of land reform were dominated by a conception of what had gone wrong in the past. The landholding village had been 'robbed' by the hacienda: therefore history must be reversed and the robbed land restored to the villages. Hence the emphasis on *restitución* (the restoration of land illegally obtained by those outside the village) as opposed to *dotación* (the taking of land, however obtained, from surrounding haciendas) as a means of forming the new peasant settlements – the *ejidos*. Restitution immediately led to difficulties over title (could the village show title?) and over the 'political' category of the village that could petition for land. Petitions would take twenty years to sort out.[3]

---

[1] Both the decree and Article 27 are printed in Manuel Fabila, *Cinco siglos de legislación agraria en México* (Mexico, 1941) p. 270; the best guide to Mexican agrarian reform as reflected in public law.

[2] This has been repeatedly pointed out by later commentators, e.g. O. Delgado (ed.), *Reformas Agrarias en la America Latina* (Mexico, 1965) esp. p. 380.

[3] Professor Karst has pointed out (St Antony's Seminars, 1968) that with all the technical difficulties involved, restitution nevertheless served a useful

L

These difficulties made it inevitable that *ejidal* land be given in *dotación*, i.e. from land taken from private landowners. Once this was clear, there began a debate between those who thought that a public sector run on communal lines (i.e. *ejidal* lands) must be fostered at the expense of private property, and those who saw in an invigorated private sector based on 'small' property the only way to secure higher production. This ideological uncertainty within the Revolutionary family was important; but even more important was the involvement of land distribution in state politics in a federal system. The whole *ejidal* structure was riddled with state politics and the creation of political clienteles. Much depended on the governor: in Zacatecas an *agrarista* who believed in *ejidos* was succeeded by a governor whose aim was to set up a kulak class.[1] Thus the emergence of a more or less national party system, and of the peasant syndicate (C.N.C.), in the 1930s was an absolute precondition of effective agrarian reform. Finally credit: in the early 1930s it was running at about 1 peso per *ejiditario*.

Thus, comparatively little land was redistributed in the early years, and President Cárdenas is rightly seen as the father of agrarian reform. It was not that he added new principles to those set out in 1915 and 1917, and which had been the subject of debate between the *agraristas* with their emphasis on greater redistribution and their more conservative opponents who favoured a 'capitalist' solution; indeed the *agraristas* had won an important victory in the debates on the Six Year Plan in December 1933 and their principles were embodied in the Agrarian Code of 1934. The main clarification affected the status of peasants living within an hacienda who, since they did not live in a settlement with political category, had been denied the right to petition for land.

What Cárdenas gave was energy, a decisive indication that a powerful national executive was determined to back the principles of agrarian reform as they had emerged from the Revolution. With Señora Cárdenas he sat in the cotton district of Torreón, and in forty-five days created the *ejidos* of La Laguna by expropriating half a million hectares. What Cárdenas proved was that agrarian reform must be impelled from above; as long as expropriation depended on the initiative of petitioning peasant communities, it tended to get bogged down in procedural wrangles. At

purpose: it gave the peasant a sense that the land was really his by a legal process. One of the great difficulties of land reform is to give the *new* peasant faith in the permanence of the new legal order that issues from revolution. This is a point much emphasized in another form by Mendieta y Nuñez.

[1] See Moises de la Peña, *Mito y realidad de la reforma agraria en Mexico* (Mexico, 1967) pp. 317 ff.

La Laguna, Cárdenas encouraged the syndicates to protest against wages and conditions, and then carried their protests to expropriation – a variation of the procedures he adopted against the foreign oil companies. He saw also, as all agrarian reformers see now, that agrarian reform was more than mere redistribution; not merely the initial push but the subsequent coddling of a weak peasant class was the duty of the state. 'Reformed' agriculture must be provided with credit and education, and there is a sense in which Cárdenas wanted the supposed paternalism of the old *hacendado* replaced by the guidance of the agronomists of the Ejidal Bank. The word 'integral' was not fashionable in the late 1930s; but it was integral agrarian reform that Cárdenas believed in, though Mexico lacked the financial resources to make it a reality.

Cárdenas was hardly a dogmatic socialist. Though he realized that agrarian reform must entail an immediate fall in production which must be accepted by a reformer, and that no agrarian reform would ever get under way if large productive units were spared merely because they were productive, he nevertheless tried to strike a balance between a highly productive private sector and a 'reformed' sector. Again, he was prepared to push the *agraristas*' collectivist solutions only where they would work, i.e. on the larger *ejidos*. His ideology was often more reminiscent of William Morris than Marx; thus he hoped to plant industry in the countryside and to connect it with the *ejidal* system. One thing Cárdenas did: he broke decisively with the idea which had appeared in 1912 – that the *ejidal* plot should be a supplementary support to a peasant who worked elsewhere. The *ejido* was to be the central institution. As we shall see on the poorer *ejidos*, the *ejidal* plot could not function as a sole support of the *ejiditario*.

After Cárdenas, the *agraristas* were less favoured. Indeed, a Japanese Marxist, Okabe, sees Cárdenas as the destroyer of feudalism who gave 'the go-ahead for capitalist development in agriculture; be it undertaken by the new agricultural bourgeoisie or by the old landlords'.[1] There can be no doubt that the emphasis shifted, after 1940, from redistribution towards investment in irrigation and roads, which tended to favour 'private' non-*ejidal* producers, and that a firm effort was made to protect what Mexicans call the 'small proprietor', i.e. holders of 100 hectares or under.

This defence of the 'small proprietor' could easily be fitted into the framework of the Revolution: it had never been the explicit aim of the

[1] Hiroji Okabe, 'Agrarian Reform in Mexico', in *The Developing Economies*, Institute of Asian Economic Affairs, Tokyo, IV, no. 2, pp. 172 ff.

Revolution to destroy private property, though some of the more radical *agraristas* argued for nationalization of the land. The rights of the 'small proprietor' within the Revolutionary settlement had been championed by such writers as Mendieta y Nunez;[1] for this school the aim of the Revolution had been to destroy the 'unproductive' large proprietors only. The small proprietors – and by 'small' it is clear that these neo-liberals mean substantial – had been unduly disturbed by the implementation of reform and the chaos and uncertainty of agrarian legislation. The defence of 'small property' triumphed in the 1947 emendation to the 1917 constitution and in the agrarian code of 1942. Once more the dual system was asserted as the basic tenet of the Revolution.

Subsequently, the emphasis has shifted back to redistribution and to attempts to make the *ejidal* system work by injections of credit. Probably population increases make redistribution a political necessity: after the mass seasonal immigration to the United States tapered off, the population growth of northern Mexico almost forced redistribution, especially since in these regions land was still available. Thus the present President of Mexico has made the biggest single distribution of land of Mexican history in Chihuahua.[2]

Thus, the agrarian structure which has seen the economic breakthrough after 1945 is a dual structure reflecting, no doubt, the pragmatism of the Mexican Revolution. It has a reformed and a non-reformed sector which function side by side.

The 'private' non-reformed sector has three main constituents:

(1) The commercial farms either owned by those who invested in commercial agriculture in the late forties – the so-called nylon farmers – or the survivals of the old haciendas run by sons who see themselves as modern entrepreneurs in a competitive market.

(2) The *rancheros* – the typical small farmers and cattle men of the north; in pre-reform days Molina Enríquez considered them the only true agriculturalists in Mexico.

(3) The *minifundistas* – peasants who own, rent or take on share-cropping leases small plots of land which provide a bare subsistence, if that.

The *ejidal* lands created over the years since 1915 fall into two classes:

---

[1] The defence of 'small' property is the main concern of his collected articles, *Politica Agraria* (Mexico, 1957).

[2] The varying emphasis given by different Presidents to redistribution is shown in Table II, p. 168.

(1) The collective *ejidos*, of which the showpieces are La Laguna and the prosperous *ejidos* of the north.

(2) The *ejidos* with individual, usually small, subsistence plots. These are more typical of the *mesa central*, and the *ejiditarios* frequently take wage work outside the *ejido*.

If we compare the results of the reformed and non-reformed sectors in terms of production, there can be little doubt that the output of the 'private' sector has risen faster than that of the 'reformed' sector. There are many reasons for this difference.

(1) All legislation (e.g. the Codes of 1934 and 1942) allowed the former landowners to keep the equivalent of 100 hectares of irrigated land. Obviously the landowner chose the best irrigated land surrounding the *casco* – i.e. the heart of the estate with the buildings and other capital equipment. Just as in Russia, the landowner hived off the bad land on the beneficiaries of reform. This is all-important, since the quality of the land varies sharply – a similar agrarian reform in a country where land is locally relatively uniform, as in Argentina, would not have similar detrimental results for the beneficiaries.

(2) What might be referred to as the Dumont effect.[1] If agrarian reform is legally possible, but if in fact it is unlikely to affect the good producer, then there is every incentive to produce well and to invest in higher production in order to strengthen the case for private property. If expropriation is a near certainty, then disinvestment will take place.[2] There is, therefore, a case for saying that a twin system like that of Mexico forces production, always provided the sword of Damocles can be imagined as, *in extremis*, falling only on the unworthy producer.

(3) Credit is easier for the private farmer than for the small *ejidal* farmer. Private banks never favour small-scale agricultural credit, least of all when the *ejidal* structure precludes seizure of land on a mortgage; the public institutions, in many critics' views, have neither had the funds nor the technique to reach the *ejidal* farmer. In the early days, the state credit institutions operated on commercial criteria, so that very little credit would reach the small man and much was never recovered. Great efforts are being made to remedy this, but it is clear that even on

[1] This is described in R. Dumont in *Lands Alive* (London, 1965) pp. 75 ff.
[2] This is usually held to have happened under Cárdenas, but there is no great evidence to support the view. Some landowners in Chile today are exhausting land which they fear will later be expropriated.

161

the *ejidos* the small man is dependent on usurious credit granted by local merchants.[1]

(4) Irrigation programmes have favoured the private farmer.

(5) The individual plots are too small on the *ejidos*, or the participant members of the collective *ejidos* are too numerous. Though legislation has consistently increased the size of the *ejidal* holdings, many remain minute.[2]

(6) Tenurial arrangements on *ejidos* are sometimes considered too stable and legally inflexible, therefore preventing the enterprising peasant from extending his holding at the expense of the unenterprising; others argue that, although the *ejidal* system freezes ownership, it is circumvented by the politically influential; the peasant has no feeling that the land is really his and that investment is 'safe'.[3]

In fact, the position on the *ejidal* sector is exactly what common sense would suppose: on good land, with reasonable plots, as on some of the northern *ejidos*, the results compare favourably with privately owned farms. There is, however, one important qualification: there is evidence that, in recent years, taking comparable factor inputs, the utilization of these inputs by *ejidal* and other small units is more efficient than in the case of large farms. The problem is that the *ejido* is struggling with a greater scarcity of factor inputs.

In the collective *ejidos*, La Laguna, the basic problem was created when occasional workers were counted in when the size of the *ejidos* was fixed by distribution amongst those entitled to lands. On top of faulty distribution, came problems of work discipline. How can you get good work from an individual *ejiditario* when his remuneration (in fact, an anticipation of total *ejidal* profits) is independent of his individual contribution in work? There are no sanctions; the *ejiditario* cannot be evicted nor can he be disciplined effectively by overseers whom he himself elects and can dismiss.[4]

---

[1] The Ejidal Bank supplies credit to only 12–15 per cent of *ejiditarios*; its funds are limited and confined to financing of cash crops.

[2] It must be remembered that there is a *minifundista* sector *outside* the *ejidal* sector; see N. L. Whetten, *Rural Mexico* (Chicago, 1948) pp. 174 ff. The present law established 10 hectares of irrigated land as the standard holding; but the distributions in the early days make the average of cultivable land held by *ejiditarios* somewhat under 6 hectares.

[3] These difficulties have been particularly emphasized in the work of Ramón Fernández y Fernández.

[4] For the problems of the La Laguna *ejidos* see Clarence Senior, *Land Reform and Democracy* (Gainesville, Florida, 1958).

It is on the poorer 'individual plot' *ejidos* that the factor inputs are at their lowest and the plight of the *ejiditarios* in provinces like San Luis Potosi is indeed deplorable. On the *ejidos* studied by Alemán,[1] 71 per cent never touch meat; half eat only two tortillas a day. There is an extraordinary labour surplus since the plots cannot absorb much labour when on dry land twenty days of four hours will keep a small plot going. The older, poor *ejidos* tend to be left out of irrigation schemes, and it is irrigation that can turn the labour input per hectare ten or more times. With minute incomes and large amounts of spare time, 87 per cent of the *ejiditario*'s income on these poor *ejidos* comes from wage work outside the *ejido*. Finally, improvements penetrate more slowly in poor areas; dramatic increases can be obtained with hybrid seed and fertilizers, but of the poorer *ejidos* (in 1964) only 5 per cent used hybrid seed.

Hence the material condition of a poor *ejiditario* may be little different from that of a peon before the Revolution. It is scarcely surprising that the peasant in Lewis's *Pedro Martínez*, though he approves of the Revolution, feels that 'things were better' under Porfirio Díaz.[2] A cynic could argue that, the 'show' *ejidos* apart, nearly half of the Mexican rural poor are imprisoned in a structure that strangely resembles the bad old days: even in *ejidos* they are suppliers of cheap labour (but now to capital intensive rather than extensive agricultural units), and equipped with holdings that cannot yield even the barest subsistence. Moreover, outside the *ejidos* is the mass of landless labourers which no redistribution reform can hope to absorb: in 1960 they numbered 3 million.[3]

It is extremely hard to give any answer to the problem set at the beginning of this paper, i.e. what have the economic effects of distributive agrarian reform been? All that can be done is to indicate the relative importance of certain variables.

The main factor in the increase of agricultural production in the recent past has been irrigation and improvements in transport, especially the former. Intensive investment in irrigation has tended to vary inversely to distribution, and has favoured the 'private' producer; when distributive zeal has waned, investment in infrastructure has tended to wax. But the age of dramatic irrigation has perhaps passed; capital costs

[1] Eloïsa Alemán, *Investigación socioeconomica directa de los ejidos de San Luis Potosi* (Mexico, 1966).

[2] Cf. R. Adams, 'Mexico since Cárdenas', in *Social Change in Latin America Today* (Council on Foreign Relations, New York, 1960) p. 327.

[3] The *total* agricultural labour force in 1910 was 3.6 million; this is some indication of the problems created by expanding population.

mount as the 'easier' schemes are completed. Now an immediate increase in production will perhaps come less from irrigation than from fertilizers and hybrid seeds.

Just as easily irrigable land is diminishing, so is, apart from tropical lands and the cattle lands of the north, the reserve of cultivable land that could profitably be distributed to *ejidos*. If little extra can be gained from further redistribution, why persist? Apart from the necessity of maintaining the myth of the ongoing Revolution, Mexican governments must always of necessity be obsessed by the problems posed by a rapidly growing population. Though the proportion of total population engaged in agriculture falls relatively, it rises absolutely. Redistribution may be one way of halting the rush to the towns and an inflated service sector, given that industry cannot conceivably absorb the constant increase in the labour force.

Nevertheless, in the poor *ejidos*, more population can be retained only by investment on marginal lands; the government limits such investment – it is patently irrational economically, however great its social benefits – and in this case the surplus must either go to the towns or to more prosperous agricultural areas.

One feature of the Revolutionary land settlement is, however, significant. As we have argued, the threat of Revolutionary land reform was not directed against private property as such but against over-large concentrations of landed property. However fluid the definition of large holdings, the great estates of the Díaz period are no more, and small property – both in its *ejidal* and private form – more widespread; this small property has contributed with some success to the domestic market in foodstuffs, as can be seen in the case of maize produced on non-irrigated land, a significant proportion of which can be assumed to be in small units: from 1·6 million metric tons (average 1934–6) production has risen to 9·02 (average for 1965–7).[1]

There is a sense in which it matters less what Revolutionary agrarian reform has achieved than what it is supposed to have achieved. Most commentators would hold that by a mixture of propaganda, myth and real achievement, the Revolutionary family which runs Mexico has at least staved off agrarian unrest: the government of the institutionalized Revolution can still maintain it is for the poor against the rich, and no serious peasant agitation has got off the ground; individual protests are bought off or hushed up; the economic demands of the C.N.C. (the

[1] For 1934–6 *Anuario Estadístico 1938*, p. 182; for 1965–7 *Revista de Estadística, 1968*.

'peasant' union) are heard, the political protest does not develop.[1] There is no need to prove how important political stability is for economic growth.

This is not to argue that the Revolution has eliminated poverty in Mexico, particularly rural poverty. The gap between rich and poor is growing and pockets of terrible poverty in the countryside are mitigated only by emigration, encouraged by the very sharp differential between rural and urban wages. Rural unemployment keeps the lower 20 per cent of the Mexican population at levels where no propaganda can convince them that they are prosperous.

It is difficult either to prove or disprove the assertion that agrarian reform as it was carried out in Mexico was a precondition of economic growth.[2] Industrial growth has come from a 'dynamic' middle class which has created and dominates a political system and a state apparatus that is willing to back its dynamism; it was the emergence of such a class – anti-foreign and devoted to the national development of Mexico – that was the ideal of such revolutionary statesmen as Carranza and Calles.[3]

This class has often been indifferent if not hostile to the reformed agrarian sector – though it is important to realize that agriculture as a whole has never been penalized at the expense of industry as happened in Perón's Argentina. Under Alemán it became fashionable to assert once more that the *ejido* was a transitional phenomenon between the latifundia and 'sensible' private property in land to be developed by modern capitalism; that it was irrational to seek directly to alleviate rural poverty which would vanish once the painful adjustments of industrialization had passed away. Yet the *ejido* has persisted as the basic rural institution and it is inconceivable that it should be abandoned even when the poorer *ejidos* have become almost an irrelevance.

Now a new problem confronts the new class. The import substitution on which it has thrived, it has been argued, has now reached a limit where either the domestic market must be expanded or there must be

[1] The extreme left and the extreme right have toyed with rather than exploited peasant discontent, e.g. Jacinto López in Sonora where he organized the squatting of landless labourers on private and *ejidal* land. The *sinarquista* movement on the extreme right tried to present the Revolutionary land settlement as a piece of hypocrisy.

[2] The assertion of Ramón Beteta, a supporter of Cárdenas and later a minister of Alemán, represents current orthodoxy. 'I believe that later prosperity would have been impossible without the social basis of greater justice which Cárdenas created' (quoted J. W. Wilkie, *The Mexican Revolution* (Berkeley, 1967) p. 90).

[3] See especially Moisés González Navarro, 'Le développement économique et social au Mexique', in *Annales*, XXI (July 1966).

a break-out into exports.[1] Since the latter is unlikely, it has been argued that industrial entrepreneurs, worried by the inelasticity of the domestic market, may become deeply concerned, in their own interests, with raising the level of rural incomes.[2] But the argument neglects what recent ECLA data reveal: that in an expanding population where the top 5 per cent and the bottom 60 per cent are losing a relative share of a growing national income, then the middle 35 per cent may be enriching themselves at a rate sufficient to provide an expansive domestic market for an indefinite future.[3] In these conditions a government whose sole criterion is economic expansion has no need to make heavy investment in an attempt to alleviate grinding rural poverty.

[1] For an early caution that industrialization could be pushed too fast, see S. Mosk, *Industrial Revolution in Mexico* (Berkeley, 1950).

[2] Cf. the observations on the domestic market in R. Vernon, *The Dilemma of Mexico's Development* (Cambridge, Mass., 1963) pp. 184 ff.

[3] I owe this important point to Mr Laurence Whitehead.

TABLE I

Index of Manufacturing and Agricultural Production
(both volume)
(1900 = 100)

Year	Index Manufacturing	Index Agriculture	Year	Index Manufacturing	Index Agriculture
1901	101·0	109·0	1933	178·5	128·9
1902	106·1	90·7	1934	266·6	114·4
1903	113·0	111·4	1935	259·4	119·8
1904	118·8	107·3	1936	298·6	133·2
1905	125·9	121·5	1937	312·6	125·0
1906	130·0	128·7	1938	321·8	127·2
1907	134·8	170·3	1939	341·3	140·6
1908	138·9	148·2	1940	358·7	134·9
1909	144·4	172·8	1941	413·7	145·0
1910	146·8	163·1	1942	472·0	158·9
1911	138·6	105·7	1943	497·6	154·6
1912	112·6	111·3	1944	535·8	160·4
1913	130·4	196·1	1945	584·3	159·0
1914	97·3	116·0	1946	595·9	166·3
1915	116·7	124·3	1947	579·2	179·0
1916	107·2	145·8	1948	625·3	198·0
1917	97·6	119·5	1949	680·5	217·5
1918	92·8	91·5	1950	778·8	238·7
1919	117·4	139·6	1951	864·5	250·9
1920	113·7	99·7	1952	929·9	241·1
1921	111·9	82·8	1953	909·6	263·5
1922	152·6	98·1	1954	976·6	320·6
1923	173·0	112·2	1955	1077·9	363·8
1924	181·2	116·5	1956	1196·2	357·3
1925	186·0	124·5	1957	1337·2	387·9
1926	211·3	141·8	1958	1415·9	429·7
1927	191·5	132·6	1959	1524·1	401·0
1928	200·3	138·8	1960	1662·7	429·5
1929	212·6	113·9	1961	1784·2	464·3
1930	223·9	104·7	1962	1907·3	487·1
1931	266·2	132·0	1963	2115·2	510·2
1932	192·8	115·2	1964	2481·3	581·1
			1965	2672·4	598·3

TABLE II

Distribution of Land by Presidential Regimes

Presidents	Periods	Hectares (1,000s)	per cent
Venustiano Carranza	1915–1920	132	0·2
Adolfo de la Huerta	May–Nov 1920	34	0·1
Alvaro Obregón	1920–1924	971	1·7
Plutarco Elias Calles	1924–1928	3088	5·5
Emilio Portes Gil	1928–1930	1173	2·1
Pascual Ortiz Rubio	1930–1932	1469	2·6
Abelardo Rodríguez	1932–1934	799	1·4
Lázaro Cárdenas	1934–1940	17890	31·6
Manuel Avila Camacho	1940–1946	5519	9·7
Miguel Alemán Valdés	1946–1952	3845	6·8
Adolfo Ruiz Cortines	1952–1958	3199	5·6
Adolfo López Mateos	1958–1964	16004	28·3
Gustavo Díaz Ordaz	1964–1966	2507	4·4
Total handed over by August 1966		56630	100·0

Index

169

For Product Safety Concerns and Information please contact our EU
representative GPSR@taylorandfrancis.com
Taylor & Francis Verlag GmbH, Kaufingerstraße 24, 80331 München, Germany